SIMON WILKIN
of
Norwich

C. B. Jewson

Centre of East Anglian Studies
University of East Anglia
1979

ISBN 0 906219 03 5

Centre of East Anglian Studies
University of East Anglia
Norwich NR4 7TJ

Contents

Illustrations

NORWICH
REFORM
FESTIVAL,
On Thursday, July 5th, 1832.

THE PROCESSION

Will form on the Castle Ditches at Eleven o'clock, and proceed from thence over Orford Hill, through Little Orford Street, the Market, London Lane, Queen Street, Tombland, over Fye Bridge, by St. Clement's Church, George's Bridge Street, Andrew's Broad Street, New Exchange Street, to the Market Place.

At Two o'Clock, the Electors friendly to Reform, will assemble on the Cricket Ground, where

A DINNER,
Of Old English Fare will be provided,
AND A PLENTIFUL
SUPPLY OF ALE.

Application having been made to allow of some Amusement and Rural Sports, the Committee have consented, and such will take place in the course of the Evening.

THE CELEBRATION OF THE DAY
WILL CONCLUDE WITH A
Display of Fireworks
SUITED TO THE OCCASION,
On the Castle Ditches.

The Committee express their anxious hope that every person will feel bound for himself to preserve the strictest order, and exert himself to maintain the same among all around him.

☞ 300 Electors Tickets, more than was contemplated by the Committee, having already been issued, the Committee can only pledge themselves to use their best exertions for the accommodation of those who may hereafter apply.

Wednesday, July 4th, 1832.

PRINTED BY WILKIN & FLETCHER, EAST ANGLIAN OFFICE, NORWICH.

Preface

Sometime before the outbreak of the last war a box
containing correspondence between Joseph Kinghorn and members of the Wilkin family was deposited in the vestry of
St Mary's Baptist Church, Norwich. I was asked to advise
what should be done with these papers. I filed the first
batch of some one hundred and fifty letters and these were
deposited with the Norwich City Library for safe keeping
and are now in the care of the Norfolk Record Office. I
was dealing with a second batch and had made notes on
another fifty documents when hostilities put an end to my
proceedings. These documents stayed in a cupboard in the
vestry and were destroyed by bombing in June 1942; only
my notes remain. So it is that for forty years I have had
an interest in the story of Simon Wilkin but it has only
been in recent times that I have been able to investigate
other aspects of his life than those revealed in the
letters and to seek other sources of information.
 Simon Wilkin is interesting as the ward (and effec-
tively the adopted son) of Joseph Kinghorn, the weight of
whose piety and learning made him a legendary figure in
Norwich during his long ministry of forty-three years at
St Mary's Baptist Church. On Kinghorn's death J.J. Gurney
wrote in his journal,
 "He was a man for whom I have long entertained a settled
 and deep esteem and a true affection. Although not without his prejudices, he was distinguished by unbending
 integrity and true piety, great learning and a very
 happy, cheerful disposition".
 From his guardian Simon inherited a firm faith in
God's providence and a clear notion of man's duty, an
inheritance which enabled him to triumph over the loss of
his fortune and to re-establish himself in life. He also
inherited a great and practical respect for learning which
flowered in his work of editing the writings of Sir Thomas
Browne and, less happily, his master's prejudices which
were ultimately to divide him from his fellow church-
members and were probably the cause of his leaving Norwich.
 This book covers the period of his life in Norwich
and, apart from detailing his not inconsiderable contribution to the life of the city, seeks to give a picture of
the Norwich background in the years leading up to the
Reform Act of 1832 and the reform of the Corporation which
followed.

I am indebted to my friends Dr A. Batty Shaw, Alec M. Cotman and Dr E.A. Ellis, to my son William Jewson, and to Dr Elinor S. Shaffer of the University of East Anglia who have read the whole or parts of my typescript and made valuable suggestions which I have been glad to adopt: also to Mrs Jill Paine who kindly made available to me letters and papers of the Fletcher family in her possession, and to Mrs Doris Eddington for copies of the correspondence between Amelia Opie and J.J. Gurney in the Friends House Library.

I have had much assistance from the staff of the Norfolk Record Office and the Norwich Local Studies Library and from a number of correspondents, particularly Dr Clyde Binfield of Sheffield University, Miss Irene Fletcher regarding the London Missionary Society, C.P. Finlayson, Keeper of Manuscripts at the Edinburgh University Library, J.F. Fuggles of the British Library information service, Mrs P. Gill of the West Sussex Record Office, Mrs P. Gilbert, Librarian of the Natural History Museum, K.C. Newton, County Archivist of Essex, and Dr E.A. Payne, C.H.

C.B. Jewson

Origins

On a cold February day in the year 1799 an orphan
boy of eight years old came to live at Mrs David's house
hard by the churchyard of St George's Colegate, Norwich.
Deep snow lay over the countryside and had been delaying
the London coaches but here in the city it was trodden
hard so that the going was more comfortable than it would
be when the thaw came. In the characteristic jumble of
Norwich streets the parish of St George's Colegate can
neither be said to have been fashionable nor otherwise.
In 1799 the Mayor, John Herring, and some twenty other
'gentlemen', manufacturers and merchants, were resident
there besides a similar number of operative weavers who
recorded their votes at the election. There were doubtless many other weavers and small tradesmen who, not being
freemen of the city, were not qualified to vote.
      Simon Wilkin, for such was the boy's name, was being
placed under the care of one of Mrs David's lodgers, the
Rev. Joseph Kinghorn, a bachelor of 33. Kinghorn who was
minister of the Baptist Church in St Mary's, two streets
away, had himself been an only child. He was a scholar of
the most exact habits but a man of great human qualities
besides. He had been well known to the boy all his life
having been an intimate friend of his late father. The new
association was to prove a happy one. Under his guidance
Simon was to grow up, after some misadventures, to play a
not insignificant part in Norwich life, to do some service
in the realms of Natural History and Literature, and to
earn a modest reference in the Dictionary of National
Biography.
      The purpose of this book is to record Simon's
personal history up to the time of his removal from Norwich
in 1834 but first it is necessary to look back and give an
account of his origins and the events that led up to his
being placed in the care of Joseph Kinghorn.
      Simon Wilkin was born at Costessey, a village
adjoining Norwich, on July 27th 1790, son of William
Wilkin Wilkin and his wife Cecilia Lucy. The Wilkins came
from Soham in Cambridgeshire and were a family of some
pretensions. In Soham parish church a tablet with a Latin
inscription commemorates Martin Wilkin (1674 - 1753) and
his wife Elizabeth Sterne. In 1743 John Sterne doubtless
a kinsman of Elizabeth's came from Soham to minister to
the Baptist Church in Norwich which at that time acquired

a property in St Mary's parish and was thereafter known as St Mary's Baptist Church. Joseph Wilkin, perhaps a grandson of Martin, married Sterne's daughter Susanna, who died at an early age. Joseph who survived her by many years remained a widower. He lived at Bowthorpe Hall and farmed extensively. His brother Simon also came to Norwich, set up as a grocer and prospered. In 1781 the freemen elected him Sheriff of the city but, being a dissenter, he refused to take the Sacrament in the Church of England and was excused the office. He retired from business in 1794 and having gone to Bath for the sake of his health died there in 1797. William Wilkin Wilkin was son of this Simon, born in 1762. He was sent to London to be educated at the Hoxton Academy under the learned Cyclopaedist, Dr Abraham Rees. In 1779 he was baptised at St Mary's. Later he spent some time in France. A long letter addressed to him in 1786 by one E. Costerton from 'chez M. le Marquis le Tourneur' speaks of

"Des bontés et des complaisances que vous avez pour nous pendant le tems vous chez à Paris".(1)

Parson Woodforde recorded in his diary meeting him on a number of occasions at Mr Priest's house in St Giles's.(2) About 1787 he married Cecilia Lucy Jacomb, a descendant of one of the ministers ejected from the Established Church in 1661. Their first child, Mary Snell Wilkin, was born in October 1788. Simon followed two years later and Lucy in 1791. W.W. Wilkin had acquired the water-mill at Costessey in 1787 and operated it in partnership with William Durrant as a flour mill.(3) When Joseph Kinghorn first came to Norwich in 1789 he stayed with the Wilkins at Costessey and soon became a close friend of the family. He and his host were both interested in mechanics and with the help of John Spaul the village locksmith they set about making a measuring-wheel and then an orrery.(4)

The friendship developed and when the Wilkins went to London in 1791 Kinghorn was left in charge of the Costessey establishment. He wrote:

"I am he [re] a kind of family chaplain and ready to help when called on and only go home as to a strange abode. 'Tis not very comfortable tho' I have all at command Mr Wilkin's house affords for he left me bundles of keys of I know not what that I might want nothing....."(5)

On another such occasion the Wilkins sent home a chest of toys which Kinghorn was charged to keep till they returned so that Mrs Wilkin could preside over its opening.(6)

When Kinghorn went to Yorkshire to see his parents he sold flour there for the Costessey mill and after he got home there was laughter about a customer who wrote to Wilkin and referred to him as "your rider". Laughter we are told was a common occurrence. At Costessey one day Kinghorn picked up a newspaper and read of the marriage of an ancient Yorkshire acquaintance whose name he would rather have expected to see in the obituary column. This led to much merriment.

"We, whose risible muscles are apt to be moved at trifles ..... had a hearty laugh and Mr W. proposed after supper that we should drink the bride and bridegroom's health

which was instantly agreed to and done with a good deal
of glee."(7)

Unhappily neither W.W. Wilkin nor his wife enjoyed
robust health. In the Spring of 1795 they took the family
to Bath in search of a cure. Wilkin wrote to Kinghorn of
his treatment:
"Starvation is ye word with me. No suppers - no wine -
tea - spirits - ving^r - medecine - infusions - &c &c &c.
Water Water ! Water ! Water! my frd that's ye secret.....
We are most fully employ'd - Tit has a French master and
I an Italian one twice a day - Waters Nr a mile off to
drink 3 times a day & twenty people to visit and receive
....."

The lessons cost 21/- for 10 which he thought not
dear.(8)

In due course the family moved on to Bristol and
then Cheltenham. Of their stay at the latter Simon was to
write years later:
"I and Mary well remembered our old lodgings, the scene
of many disagreeable sensations on account of the ill
temper of Miss Wells, the old maid whose were the
lodgings, added to my father's severity."(9)

That September after their return to Costessey the
family suffered an attack of scarlet fever. Mary escaped
and Simon recovered but little Lucy was carried off. This
naturally upset Mrs Wilkin whose health was delicate at
the best of times. Next Spring she was still being treated
by Dr Lubbock. The summer failed to restore her. Her
husband took the family to Cromer hoping the sea air would
do her good. Kinghorn spent a few days with them there
early in September but in the following week Mrs Wilkin
succumbed to her weakness and died.(10)

Joseph Kinghorn continued in close touch with
W.W. Wilkin. He wrote in June (1798) that they two laughed
heartily at the Rev. Andrew Fuller (Baptist Minister of
Kettering and Secretary of the Baptist Missionary Society)
being "DuncifieD" by an American College.

Not long after this Wilkin married again. Despite
this he seems to have had a premonition that his time would
not be long. At the end of August he executed a will
making provision for the care of his children in the event
of his death. Some months later he told Kinghorn that he
had confided Simon to his care - no one else, he said, so
well knew his plans. He should like him to educate his son
and would esteem it a mark of friendship if he would do it.
Kinghorn replied that they must do such things for one
another in society but he thought his own life uncertain,
his frame being weak. This caused Wilkin to add a codicil
to the will to the effect that if Kinghorn died before
Simon was 21 the boy should go to the Rev. Michael Maurice,
Presbyterian Minister and schoolmaster of Normanston near
Lowestoft, the father of F.D. Maurice.

That December W.W. Wilkin was attacked by a cold and
a complaint in his bowels and in January 1799 he died.
Kinghorn wrote to his father:
"I had told you his health was in a bad state..... He
declined, got worse, alarmed his friends by his appearance, called in medical aid, principally I believe to

3

satisfy them, at length he sank and died Jany 10, late at night..... He has left a young widow and 2 fine children to deplore what is irreparable..... He expected his end and was calm and resigned. He expressed a hope he knew in whom he had believed and had no fears of the result. I have lost a sincere friend, yet his death may be all for the best. I should have felt it much more if it had taken place some years ago. He had greatly lost his activity and utility."(11)

REFERENCES

1. Wilkin Papers (3)
2. *The Diary of a Country Parson*, Vol. II, pp.110, 293, 342
3. T.B. Norgate, *History of Costessey*, p.12
4. Martin Hood Wilkin, *Joseph Kinghorn of Norwich*, p.164
5. Kinghorn Letters, 683. J.K. to D.K. 19 September 1791
6. Wilkin Papers, 10. W.W.W. to J.K. 11 November 1794
7. Kinghorn Letters, 793. J.K. to D.K. 11 February 1794
8. Wilkin Papers, 12. W.W.W. to J.K. 6 May 1795
9. Wilkin Papers, 31. S.W. to J.K. 29 July 1810
10. Kinghorn Letters, 884. J.K. to D.K. 27 September 1796
11. Kinghorn Letters, 973. J.K. to D.K. 19 January 1799

Childhood

So Simon spent his childhood with Joseph Kinghorn
in loco parentis. The arrangement proved a happy one for
both parties. Kinghorn wrote that he had trembled at the
charge but:
"now it is come my mind is quite reconciled to it tho'
I know it will be difficult. The other Exrs. - Joseph
Wilkin, William Durrant, and William Unthank, a gentleman of the law - are ordered by the will to make me an
annual compensation which shall be sufficient and handsome. Simon is a fine boy, and left in my hands I dare
say I shall soon love him. Mary is to be educated by
Mrs Wilkin, whom Mr W. thought competent to it, and I
hope she is..."(1)
Three weeks later he wrote again:
"I do not think there is any need for anxiety about my
taking Simon. He is likely to be no trouble for a long
time. What he may be when he grows up and begins to
think himself a gentleman there is no saying. But
sufficient for the day is the evil of it. At present
he is a very pleasing boy; he will need government but
is governable. He is a little fellow, very volatile, or
what will better charactise him, he is a great monkey.
His powers are considerable and I hope we shall do very
well together..... He is quite willing to come to me and
has made a number of diverting childish stipulations,
most of w^c. have been agreed to."(2)
Kinghorn as we have seen was lodging in St George's
at the house of Mrs David, his predecessor's widow. He
shared these lodgings with William Youngman, a Suffolk man
who after training with grandfather Simon Wilkin, was now
in business on his own account. Simon remembered him
afterwards as a man of extensive reading and varied information, vigorous intellect and great conversational
powers. He was descended from the Meadows family and thus
connected with the Taylors and Martineaus of the Octagon
Chapel but was himself a member of the Independent Old
Meeting.(3) He was to take an increasingly active part in
the affairs of the city and will appear again in our story.
Room was found for Simon at Mrs David's. With him came
about half his father's library which was not so easily
accommodated. Kinghorn complained that his room was so
lumbered up with books that there was no stirring. He
thought he might have to move to accommodate the boy better.

At this time Kinghorn's mind was preoccupied with another anxiety. For twenty-nine years his father had ministered to the little Baptist cause at Bishop Burton near Beverley in Yorkshire. Now there had arisen differences between him and the leading members of his flock and it was plainly expedient for him to leave. Joseph urged him to come to Norfolk and this was in due course agreed upon. David and Elizabeth Kinghorn arrived in Norwich in July 1799. Simon who had now been four months in residence with his guardian recollected the incident fifty years later when he wrote:

"Just after we had dined and I was about to resume my studies, a messenger arrived with a note; and Mr Kinghorn suddenly and under some excitement rose to leave the house. On my eager enquiry he told me that his father and mother had arrived...... and that he was going to meet them. .... At length they arrived and I was summoned to the interview. .... I had never seen a couple who so struck my boyish imagination. Nor was I received with indifference, expecially by Mrs Kinghorn. .... Her appearance and manners at once attracted me. Her figure was short and plump. She wore an ample cloak of black satin lined with ermine; and a white round cap edged with lace peeped from under a large round bonnet also of black satin. Her countenance, accent and manner were full of kindness and gentleness and she won my heart at once. But her partner struck me with much surprise and with something like awe. He was very tall and sturdily upright. His hat with a round and very shallow crown, and broad upturned verge, rested on an ample white full-bottomed wig. His upper dress was of dark blue; the coat of great length and amplitude with copious sleeves, large buttons and wide-flapped pockets. .... His nether dress was of black velvet buckled at the knees with dark gray stockings terminated by square-toed substantial shoes and large square buckles. His countenance was remarkably robust and even rubicund; with keen grey eyes and shaggy brows; expressive of shrewdness and great determination. But though of aspect somewhat formidable to a child he addressed me with such quaint and lively kindness as at once to reassure me. My first interview was highly interesting and further acquaintance ripened into a strong affection towards them both."(4)

The coming of the senior Kinghorns had an effect unfortunate from our point of view - it terminated the regular correspondence between father and son from which we might have learned much about Simon's early life and development.

Having Simon under his wing Joseph Kinghorn was pressed to take other pupils. He turned down four, being, he said, "more covetous of time than guineas". He was already tutoring William Hawkins, son of Thomas Hawkins the grocer and deacon of St Mary's, who thus became Simon's playmate. William later went on to Edinburgh University and after graduating there became a Baptist Minister.

About a year after Simon joined him Kinghorn

6

decided to set up house on his own and searched for one
suitable to the modest needs of his ward and himself.
This he found in Pottergate, a narrow street running from
the Maddermarket in the centre of the city westwards. At
its western end, just within the city wall, Pottergate
broadened into St Benedict's Plain. This plain remained
little changed until recent years when bombing and slum-
clearance removed many of its picturesque buildings. On
the North was a terrace of solid Georgian houses with sash
windows and classical doorways. On the West a medieval
building with numerous angles, gables and chimneys, giving
the appearance of growth rather than design, faced East
down Pottergate. On the South another block of ancient
houses formed three sides of a shallow rectangle. One of
these Kinghorn hired, a little plastered house of two
stories and an attic, with a pair of gables on either side,
facing North to the street and South to its garden.
Beside the house lilies of the valley grew between the
pebbles of a pavement. Then the garden sloped up the hill
with celery beds and scarlet runners on one side and on
the other a grass plot with an old mulberry tree in the
middle. Above this the garden ended in a melée of horse-
radish and currant bushes. Beyond were the backs of the
houses lining St Giles's and Cow Hill with the tall black
flint tower of St Giles's church rising above them whose
bells would ring out on national occasions and at such
times as anyone saw fit to subsidise the ringers. The
study on the first floor facing the garden and the garden
itself were Kinghorn's especial domains. The rest of the
house with the housekeeping and the care of Simon's ward-
robe became the province of a housekeeper, Eleànor Cutting,
who was to continue in that capacity for the remaining 32
years of Kinghorn's life. She acknowledged the preeminence
of her master in matters of religion, accepted his opinions
and was baptised at St Mary's in November 1800. But in
domestic affairs no doubt she reigned supreme.
   Simon visited Costessey from time to time, sometimes
on his own, sometimes in the company of his guardian, but
it soon became apparent that he was happier in his new
abode than Mary was with her step-mother. Early in 1801
she somehow contrived to join her brother. Mrs Wilkin
seems not to have been sorry to part with her though she
wrote an indignant letter complaining of a tale circulated
at the William Taylors' and Thomas Martineaus' that she had
ill-treated the child.(5) Mary was in due course placed in
the care of Mrs Durrant, the widow of a Norfolk clergyman,
living in a house in St George's opposite that occupied by
John Crome.(6)
   Some time after the move to Pottergate, William
Hawkins's sister Anne also became one of Kinghorn's pupils.
Years afterwards she transmitted an account of the scene
to her step-daughter Cecilia Lucy Brightwell:
   "Hither did mother now betake herself each day from 9
till 12 to study algebra, astronomy and arithmetic.
Above-stairs at the study window she was planted with
Simon for her vis-à-vis, she with the hated slate, he
poring over his books and the Reverend in his blue stuff
gown absorbed in his studies. Silently the group pursued

their different objects until 11, when the Reverend,
closing his books gave his attention to his pupils".(7)
      At noon the party broke off their studies and went
out for a walk. For some years this followed an invariable route - one mile along the Dereham turnpike and
back. So exact was the timing of this operation that it
served as a signal to a cottage on the route where the
order was regularly given 'Put on the 'tatoes, here come
the tall gentleman.'(8)
      While the routine of the classroom went on with calm
and unfailing regularity, the children cannot have been
entirely unaware of the events going on beyond its walls.
They were taught to believe that they were under the care
of a benevolent Providence and whatever might come to pass
must be accepted and would surely work out for their good.
There were no hourly or even daily news-media to innoculate
them against the effect of what they heard but the city was
news-conscious in a manner unknown to us. When a coach
from London was expected to bring news of a notable event
it would be greeted by crowds as it entered the city and
if the news were sufficiently momentous the bells in the
three-dozen steeples would be set ringing. Napoleon was
the ogre of the time and his invasion plans the preoccupa-
tion of leading citizens. In 1802 rejoicings greeted the
peace of Amiens, marked by a brilliant illumination of the
city. The whigs and radicals, with whom Kinghorn sympa-
thised, though he considered it inappropriate to take an
active part in political affairs, had always been opposed
to the war but when in 1803 France once more declared war
there was a remarkable unanimity of agreement on the
necessity of standing up to the threat. William Taylor,
the prophet of the radicals and enthusiast for the French
Revolution, wrote in his paper, the Iris,
  "A spirit of loyalty is very prevalent in the city. A
  majority of all ranks are anxious to be trained in the
  use of arms. .... We congratulate our fellow-citizens".(9)
      A volunteer regiment of infantry was formed in
Norwich with several of the hitherto pacifists among its
officers. Whigs and tories equally entered into a subscription in support of the project. Marsh and Sons, the
Norwich carriers, offered for the service of the government
in case of invasion their fleet of one hundred horses,
twelve broadwheeled waggons, and twenty four boats with
forty men and three boys to service them, while Lady
Jerningham of Costessey proposed to raise and command a
corps of six hundred females to drive away cattle from the
sea-coast. Simon must often have seen the marching and
drilling of the volunteers and perhaps witnessed the
stirring occasion when the Mayor presented them with their
colours - painted by James Sillett with the City arms -
and their commander, Lieutenant Colonel Harvey, addressed
them with the words,
  "Volunteers! I trust you whilst sword or bayonet remains
  among us to defend your colours".
      Happily the volunteers were never called upon to
display their valour but the war dragged on and news was
seldom encouraging. In November 1805 the schoolroom must
have been enlivened by the joyful ringing of St Giles's

bells when tidings of the victory of Trafalgar reached the
city. They were to ring again a sad toll on January 9th
1806, the day when Nelson's remains were interred in St
Paul's. Perhaps Simon was taken to see the moving panorama
representing Nelson's funeral which was later exhibited at
Harper's Pantheon. Kinghorn's puritan proclivities forbad
the stage and the reading of fiction but other forms of
entertainment presented themselves in the established
routine of the city's year. Tombland Fair came at Easter-
tide with its swings and roundabouts and spectacles of
dwarfs or other unusual figures, and then the diet would
be varied by the traditional Fair Buttons, brown and white
spiced biscuits. In June was Guild Day when the install-
ation of a new Mayor was an occasion for civic pageantry.
Standard bearers in gay clothes and mitre-like head-gear
led the procession. The Mayor in robes and chain was
preceded by the sword-bearer with his Tudor cap and mace-
bearers carrying the shining golden maces. The procession
was enlivened by the presence of Snap, the canvas dragon,
last relic of the medieval pageant of St George, who kept
the boys at bay by threatening to pull off their caps with
his gnashing iron jaws. In August came Assize week when
the society of the county visited Norwich and there were
a series of concerts and exhibitions and events in the
Public Gardens included fire-work displays. Twelve Night,
after Christmas was celebrated by the Pastry-cooks whose
shops were decorated and illuminated for the occasion and
on Valentine's eve in February parcels for the children
were left anonymously on the doorsteps, the donors peeling
the door-bell and running for cover.
    Some years before Simon joined him Joseph Kinghorn
had acquired a microscope and his interest in Natural
History was soon passed on to his ward. No doubt this
interest would be further stimulated by visits to the
travelling exhibitions and menageries which came to the
city fairly frequently. For instance Bullock's celebrated
Cabinet of Curiosities was displayed in three commodious
rooms in the Gentlemen's Walk in November 1799 - 'There
never was such a collection in Norwich before', said the
Mercury. The collection included a Museum of Natural and
Foreign Curiosities collected by the most famous Circum-
navigators - birds, beasts, fishes and reptiles; dresses,
arms and war-like instruments. Bullock's 'cabinet' also
displayed wax figures, large as life - the late King,
Queen and Dauphin of France; the French General Buonaparte;
Richard Parker the mutineer and Tippoo Sahib with his two
sons.
    Mr Polito's collection of living foreign beasts was
sometimes to be seen at the Duke's Palace Yard, sometimes
on Hog Hill. From time to time his caravans carried the
Striped Bengal Tiger, the Laughing Hyena, the Ravenous
Wolf, the Pelican of the Wilderness, the Grand Cassowary
from Java and many more strange creatures. In December
1806 he brought what he claimed was the only male lion
travelling in His Majesty's dominions. 'This astonishing
animal', his advertisement reads,
    'has limbs superior in size and strength to any horse or
ox. He is accompanied by a beautiful Pointer bitch whom

9

he was suckled by and now shews not only great affection
for but suffers her quite to rule over him.'
    So the boy grew up in a lively city. He was always
to look back on a happy childhood.

REFERENCES

1. Kinghorn Letters, 973. J.K. to D.K. 19 January 1799
2. Kinghorn Letters, 977. J.K. to D.K. 15 February 1799
3. M.H. Wilkin, op. cit. p.279
4. M.H. Wilkin, op. cit. p.4 & 5
5. C.B.J. Notes 3
6. C.L. Brightwell, *Life of Mr Brightwell of Norwich*,
   1869 p.26
7. C.L. Brightwell, M.S.69, Norfolk Record Office
8. M.H. Wilkin, op. cit. p.312
9. Iris, 30 July 1803

Beginning to think himself a Gentleman

In July 1808 Simon accompanied Kinghorn on a visit
to Ebenezer Hollick at Whittlesford Lodge near Cambridge.
Kinghorn described the visit in a letter to his father:
"We have seen at Cambridge colleges, chapels, paintings,
&c &c &c, till for my part I was tired of seeing. We
have seen the famous Codex Bezae..... We have seen a
manuscript Hebrew Bible written about the year 846.....
We were in Dr Long's orrery, which is repaired and much
improved since I saw it before. We have on the whole
seen the best arguments I have met with for a long time
for the establishment, which are the ample provisions
made for its members; and the impression of which must
be great on the minds of those whose prejudices and early
habits attach them to a church which has so many other
charms....."
Their fellow guests included Dr Abraham Rees whom
Simon thought a splendid person, dignified and courteous,
yet full of conversation and information.(1)
During the stay at Whittlesford Simon celebrated
his eighteenth birthday. Mary was already nineteen and
Kinghorn was concerned to see them both settled with
satisfactory partners. Among his papers was a letter from
a young man, H. Perkins of Tofts, protesting his love for
Mary but fearing that his letter would be intercepted. It
evidently was. Happily Mary had formed a firm attachment
to Thomas Brightwell, a young lawyer whom she had met when
staying with kinsmen. Ebenezer Hollick had a daughter
Caroline and the elders fell to projecting a match with
Simon. The idea was not unpleasing. A few months later
Simon sent her a present but in the end nothing came of it.
Simon now became deeply devoted to the study of
insects, an interest which brought him into touch with
other naturalists. At Michaelmas 1808 he met A.H. Haworth,
a notable enthusiast in this field. Kinghorn, Joseph
Hooker - elder brother of W.J. Hooker, later of Kew - and
John Burrell, the entomologist Vicar of Letheringsett,
were all present at this encounter when Haworth and Simon
agreed on an exchange of specimens and appointed Burrell
and Hooker to arbitrate in case they failed to agree on the
relative value of the exchanges. This led to a facetious
letter from Burrell to Kinghorn asking him to remind Wilkin
to submit his list of items to him as umpire.
Simon had serious interests too. In October 1808

he was baptised by Kinghorn on profession of his faith and
became a member of the church at St Mary's in whose affairs
he was to take an active part. He came of a Baptist family
- his father and grandfather had been Baptists - but it
required a personal decision for him to become a Baptist
himself. It is then necessary for us to pause in our
narrative to give some account of the peculiarities and
origins of the Baptist denomination and its condition at
the time of Simon's joining it. Baptists were distinguished from other Christian bodies by their rejection of Infant
Baptism and their insistance on the baptism (by immersion)
of believers who had made a profession of faith. Such
they believed was the only form of Baptism known to the
New Testament. Their continuous history originated with
men who adopted and embodied these views in the seventeenth century. The Baptist churches in Norfolk had grown
out of the Puritan movement. From the reign of Elizabeth
onwards there were Puritan nonconformists within the
established church in Norwich diocese. When Matthew Wren
became bishop in 1635 he set out to uproot such nonconformity. His proceedings led to several clergy taking
refuge in the Netherlands, to be followed by a considerable
number of lay supporters. In Holland they learned how to
organise churches on a Congregational basis as defined by
Dr William Ames in his *Medulla Theologia*. In 1642 after
the calling of a 'hopeful Parliament' - known to us as the
Long Parliament - they thought it safe to return and set up
churches here, churches which were comprehended in the
loose establishment of the Commonwealth. Among these
churches Baptist views began to be held and inevitably
proved a divisive force. By 1646 there was a church at
Pulham which 'dissented from the Baptism of Infants'.
After the Restoration the Norwich Congregationalists were
ejected from the church of St George Tombland which they
had hitherto occupied and became an illegal body. Soon
after this the Baptists among the membership of this
church, some of whom had been among the refugees in the
Low Countries, drew apart from the rest and when in 1669
Bishop Edward Reynolds, made a return to the Archbishop
of illicit congregations meeting in his diocese he reported
this and five other churches in Norfolk as 'anabaptist
conventicles'. This Norwich 'anabaptist conventicle' was
the church which in 1745 settled in St Mary's parish and
which Simon was now joining. The Baptist Churches were
divided doctrinally into two wings; the Particular Baptists
- to which the church in St Mary's belonged - adhering to
the Calvinism which had been the orthodoxy of the Puritans
and the early Reformers of the Church of England; and the
General Baptists, espousing the Arminian doctrine, who also
had a church in Norwich. Calvinists emphasised the pre-
dominance of God's action; Arminians the free-will of man.
The Baptists inclined to be conservative in doctrine as
was Joseph Kinghorn though he was aware of the 'higher
critism' of the Scriptures being pursued by German theo-
logians. He learned German in order to read Eichhorn's
'Einleitung ins Alten Testament' and other works.
    The romance beteen Mary Wilkin and Thomas Brightwell
took time to mature. She had first met him in 1806 but it

was not till the end of 1809 that Kinghorn thought it
necessary to apply to S. Daniel, the Colchester lawyer to
whom Thomas had been articled, as to his talents, character, religious sentiments and prospects. The reply was
satisfactory. In January 1810 Simon went to Woodbridge to
visit his prospective brother-in-law. He wrote an account
of the visit in a letter to his guardian. He had left
Norwich early, breakfasting at Wacton about 9.15 and
dining at Ipswich at 3.30. Thence a pleasant ride in the
dusk to Woodbridge where the lodgings were satisfactory
having a pleasant parlour and a neat garden. Next morning
the two young men walked to the barracks to serve a writ
on a German officer. The officer had gone but the expedition enabled Simon to gather a rare plant and to see some
of the soldiers, who, he wrote, seemed -
    "enough to make poor skinny frog-fed Frenchmen quake
    should they pay us a visit - which however God forbid!
    for after all we must be in a dreaful situation in the
    event of an Invasion...."
    He cannot think what possesses the British Ministry
to persist in a fruitless struggle to uphold a tottering
monarchy against so vast superiority as Buonaparte
possesses.
    "God.... has yet some unaccomplished Designs to fulfil.
    May not our Subjugation be of the Number. Be that as
    it may however we have a Mansion prepared for us where
    we shall for ever dwell undisturbed by rumours of War -
    May we be fitted for it."(2)
    Brightwell wrote of the visit,
    "We found each other congenial companions, especially in
    our mutual love of Natural History. I well remember his
    ardour and youthful zeal in religion. He was exceedingly
    busy in organising a choir of singers at Mr Kinghorn's
    chapel and was indefatigable in pricking out notes of
    hymn tunes; an occupation which.... engaged a good deal
    of his time while with me."(3)
    In April 1810, in his twentieth year, Simon began
to take part in the public life of the city. Joseph Lancaster had visited Norwich that March, lecturing at the
Theatre and at the Maid's Head Inn on his system of
education. Lancaster who was a thriftless, impulsive and
extravagant character but had a gift for teaching, had
started a school in the Borough Road, Southwark, and having
no means to pay teachers had evolved a monitorial system
whereby the elder scholars taught the younger. His
activities received a great fillip when the King sent for
him and told him, 'It is my wish that every poor child in
my dominions should be taught to read the Bible'. His
finances being in disarray, some Quaker friends paid his
debts and his school was made over to trustees and
designated 'the Royal Lancasterian Society'. Though the
Norfolk Chronicle criticised Lancaster for censuring his
'fellow labourers' - teachers who worked on other lines
than his - he made sufficient impression for a meeting to
be arranged with a view to putting his ideas into practice
in Norwich. This was held in the Guildhall on April 17th
1810. The meeting put Joseph Gurney in the chair and
resolved to set up a Lancasterian school for boys aged six

13

to twelve. Simon was evidently present; he was appointed
a member of the committee set up to carry out the scheme,
with J.J. Gurney, John Pitchford (a Roman Catholic),
Jonathon Davey (a prominent politician and property
developer), William Taylor (the German scholar) and other
leading citizens. Two of the Gurneys donated each thirty
guineas to the project and Simon's enthusiasm may be
guaged from the fact that while most of the well-to-do
supporters were content to give two guineas, a few of them
five, he donated ten and persuaded his sister Mary to do
the same.(4) A property was acquired in St Martin's at
Palace and the school opened there a year later with
upwards of 250 boys, paying a penny a week for their
education.

Later that April (1810) Simon accompanied his future
brother-in-law on an expedition to London. They stayed at
the New Hummums, a hotel in Covent Garden.

"The accommodations here," he wrote, "are excellent -
but the Piazzas in sight of the House are full of bad
Company. .... It is scarcely possible to pass thro' any
of the larger Streets unmolested by girls of the Town."

At the British Museum they met William Elford Leach,
a young man of Simon's age, who had permission to 'copy
insects' there. With him they made a trip across the
Thames to Battersea where they landed amid gardens and
cultivated grounds, examining trees, stones, plants and
every moving thing in search of treasures. Leach introduced them to Pierre-André Latreille, the French entomologist who had recently published his *Genera Crustaceorum et
Insectorum* and was then visiting London. Brightwell
recorded that he talked in French and was fully engaged in
examining the collections of insects under Leach's care.
Leach told them that Latreille's memory was so good that
when he had once examined any insect he never needed to
have any subsequent recourse to it and that his own
collections were kept in the utmost disorder, stuck in
hat-boxes or whatever came to hand.(5)

Simon visited the Liverpool Museum, containing
"beautiful and rare things but many unscientific impos-
tures"; Miss Linwood's Exhibition of Needlework -- "some
fine pictures all done in Worsted" -- and James Sowerby's
famous natural history collection.

Nelly Cutting had evidently expressed anxiety about
her charge being exposed to the dangers of London. He
wrote to his guardian,

"Tell Nelly I am perfectly safe and in health tho' in
London -- & let me know how is her throat."(6)

In June 1810 Mary Wilkin and Thomas Brightwell were
married. They set out on their wedding tour accompanied
by Simon and by Ann Hawkins. Travelling at a leisurely
speed they reached Bury St Edmunds for the first night and
thence went on to London, staying at the York Hotel in
Bridge Street, Blackfriars. Simon, having visited London
before, was somewhat blasé. He wrote:

"Once more to my no small annoyance have I entered this
dismal dungeon called the stupendous Metropolis of the
British Empire..... My sister is just saying that from
the view she has yet had of it..... she thinks it about

the filthiest place she could conceive of.... Mrs B.
after tea going to the window... burst out laughing and
calling out to me exclaimed 'What an inconceivable
fright is that bundle who walks there?' I most gravely
and with perfect nonchalence, answered 'Oh 'tis only a
Turk'. The immense hat of a drayman next excited her
attention and merriment. Thus the varied scenes from
the window afforded her & Ann continual amusement -
while I in the most horrible pouting fit sat solemnly
journalising at a table. Meanwhile at another table sat
my Brother busily employed in making a list of Lions."(7)
    In London Simon found himself involved in the
politics of the Baptist denomination. It was proposed to
establish an academy in London to train young men for the
ministry. Joseph Gutteridge, a leading London Baptist,
had written to Kinghorn inviting him to become Principal
Tutor. Kinghorn had turned down the request but Gutteridge
was disinclined to take 'no' for an answer. The Rev. James
Dore, minister of Maze Pond Baptist Church, begged Simon
to give him an hour's interview. He suggested that perhaps
Gutteridge's approach had not been the most tactful and
that more information ought to have been given. Kinghorn
would, he said, be Divinity and Classical Tutor and
possibly Housekeeper with an allowance of so much per
student. The salary might be £400 per annum. All this
Simon reported in a letter home.(8)
    The wedding party went on to the Isle of Wight and
then to the West country. At Exeter they were in difficulty because the order from Barclay and Co. for their
money requirement had not reached the local bank. Nevertheless -
"We reached Glastonbury on Wednesday evening. The
approche is beautiful. The ruins of the abbey engaged
and by their grandeur and beauty fully repaid our
attention next morning.... It was shewn by a blind man
who was led by a boy. We left on Thurs. [July] 19th and
reached Bath about sunsett. It is an incomparably more
elegant city than any I ever saw. If London be the
metropolis of Commerce and Wealth, Bath may justly claim
the title of the metropolis of Elegance and Fashion. Its
Royal Crescent is superior to any Place in London....."
    They left Bath on the Saturday for Bristol and the
same evening called on Dr Ryland, Principal of the Baptist
Academy, where Joseph Kinghorn had received his education.
On Sunday they heard the Doctor preach - "but with little
interest". On Monday they breakfasted with him and he
shewed them the library and the catalogue which Kinghorn
had made in his student days.
"The Dr accused it of blunders wh put me in a great rage.
I insisted on clearing up the matter when at last I found
it had been continued by a Welshman and some part transcribed by him. Therefore I appeased myself by agreeing
to impute the mistakes to the poor blundering Cambrian."
    They saw the sights around Bristol and then -
"We slept at Chepstow on Tuesday and the next morning
took the Boat to Tintern Abbey. We dined off some cold
meat we had taken with us, within the Abbey walls. The
ruins are not so extensive but more elegant and

15

interesting than those at Glastonbury. We took a sketch
or two & returned to Chepstow. Next morg Thursday we
went to Gloucester, dined, saw the pin manufactory and
went on to Cheltenham..... The Pump Room I remembered
very well but did myself no good by taking half a glass
of the waters."

At Cheltenham they celebrated Simon's twentieth
birthday by reading Sir Walter Scott's new poem, *The Lady
of the Lake* . That day too Simon received a letter from
Kinghorn with the welcome news of his final declension of
the invitation to London. He wrote to his guardian from
Oxford on July 29th that the party hoped to be home in
about ten days time -

"Tho' we are coming home so soon I must request you to
drop me a letter by Friday's post to Cambridge where we
shall spend next Sunday - for so seldom are you and I
absent f^m each other long that I am covetous of y^r
letters. What do you think my d^r Sir I have just been
buying for you? A barometer. On the new plan which
seems to be ingeniously contrived and is said to be on
a more accurate principle of the old one."(9)

During this tour Simon, who would inherit his
father's fortune in a year's time, began to consider his
future and set down his thoughts in a letter to Kinghorn:
"I know something in point of literature. Tho' even
that knowledge but shews how much more must be acquired
to give me a shadow of pretension to the character of
a 'Literary Character' - I have a predilection for the
Languages, I dislike Mathematics & know nothing of the
Sciences more abstruse - Metaphysics and Logic - To mix
with those who will probably share my future acquaintance I must extend my range much wider if not much
deeper.

But all this will add nothing to my property....
s^d I marry, & s^d I have a family & s^d that family be
large.... what is £20 000 to divide among that family?"

He ought, he thought, to try to live within his
income and if possible to increase it. He knew nothing of
trade and did not relish the idea of it. All the same he
might apply himself to the milling business at Costessey
and try to establish another in a more lucrative situation
near London. In the Isle of Wight on his recent visit he
had found innumerable sources of amusement. He would like
to spend a summer there to investigate its birds, animals,
insects, plants and antiquities and to produce a popular
work, "A Summer in the Isle of Wight". His guardian, he
was sure, would laugh at the idea. Probably he did - in
any case it was not pursued.(10)

Back in Norwich that September Simon and his
brother-in-law were elected to the committee of the Public
Library. Simon did not attend its meetings very regularly
but nine months later he was appointed to an important
sub-committee with the President John Pitchford, Dr Reeve,
J.J. Gurney and Mr Geldart to inspect the stock of books
and superintend the printing of a new catalogue.

His interest in entomology now brought him into
touch with one of the most notable natural-historians in
the region, the Rev. William Kirby, Vicar of Barham near

Ipswich, who had achieved an international reputation by his book *Monographia Appium Angliae*. W.J. Hooker, who was a regular correspondent of Kirby's and had been his guest at Barham, perhaps effected the introduction. At this time Kirby was engaged in compiling the *Introduction to Entomology* in conjunction with William Spence of Hull. They followed the arrangement of Latreille's *Genera Crustaceorum et Insectorum* but as many of the insects described could not be placed in his genera, new generic names and characters were invented for them. Kirby, who was an efficient parish priest and an ardent minister of the gospel, regarded his enthusiasm for natural history as helping to display the wisdom of God in creation; he had a firm conviction that no interpretation of the Book of Nature could be correct if it militated against the true interpretation of the Word of God in the Scriptures. In September (1810) Simon went to Barham to stay with the worthy vicar. He wrote home a lively account of his adventures.

                          "Barham Tuesday evg. Sept 21.1810

Behold me now solemnly seated in an antique arm chair, in Dom Kirby's Library, solus to send you secundum desiderium - an account of me & my hitherto proceedings. I did not set off so early as I intended & I am greatly afraid my characteristic bustle of getting under weigh disturbed you. The appearance of the vehicle provided for me was wretched. It was ragged, dirty, low, unusually heavy and with no Box. Incipium malorum!! Into it I was fain, though with grumbling to mount. I lamented its ponderosity for my animal's sake; its want of stowage on account of my huge parcel. Its height for my driving and its rags and dirt for what? I suppose for my pride's sake! At length I believe I reflected that it was too bad to be mistaken for my own, therefore would scarcely expose me to ridicule. Thus I consoled myself and set off with wary steps and slow, not to fatigue my horse. I was in two minds whether to breakfast with Geo. Watson Esq." [of Saxlingham]. "I had determined to do so but could not change any one of my one pounders, therefore had nothing to give his servant, which I did not choose to omit, lest I should expose myself to his or madam's imputation of meaness, a vice which, tho' inherent in them, displeases them much, when observed in others. This foible is not a rarity in human nature. Cavendum mihi.

     As I could get no change I went on to Wacton and breakfasted. Here I could not change but obtained credit and when I had given the hostler sixpence, was unable to pay the next gate. However there I found 20 sixpences and ten shillings which sett me up. I dined at Thwaite and arrived at Barham in time to dress for dinner. Mrs K. was not at home but Miss K. an "O.M." officiated at table. Here we had Mrs Ripper, Mother of Mrs K. a venerable wreck - Blind and decrepid but still full of cheerfulness. She joins eagerly in the news of the neighbouring villages - hears of marriages, enquires about neighbour this who has the rhoumatiz neighbour to'ther who has got the going fever or the bowel complaint which seems everywhere predominant - demands an enumeration of the present at the card party which meets at various houses in the neighbourhood - and displays an astonishing readiness to relate particulars of the history of every name mentioned. When I arrived neither Mr nor Mrs K. came directly; the old lady was sitting in her easy chair; she named me, welcomed me, enquired after my health, my friends, journey, where I had rested and what hour I sett off. In short kept me talking 'till Mr K. appeared. ....

As yet I have had but little talk but Ent[l]. At tea I hauled in the writers of 17 Cent[y] whose works he says are favorites with him - has a good many of them. Admires their solidity. Thinks Leslie a good arguer. Remarking the patience of martyrs he says 'Human nature, eadem eadem ac olim, but is not now called upon to bear such trials. Nor could it then vi sua have done it but was strengthened from above. Nor does he see any doubt but if we should be placed in difficulties we could by taking right means obtain help from God.' He begins family worship starting by a kind of Invocatory address to the Almighty - then 'Let us confess our sins - when kneeling he read a kind of collect concluding with pat. nos.' Then responses standing - I remember one part - The noble army of martyrs praise thee, &c. This done 'Let us pray'. Then a prayer and thanksgiving ended with the usual benediction finishes the whole.

We this day rode to Offton, Mr Sheppard's, where I got some good insects and saw a pleasant and sensible young man. He almost gives up insects now.

After dinner 'The King' is given, which I drink vix sine grimacibus. Mr K. now comes to put an end to my scrawl. Time over. Sends respects to you. I am yours affectionately, Simon Wilkin."(11)

In December (1810) Kinghorn was in London and Simon staying at the Brightwells' new establishment at Thorpe next Norwich. He wrote to his guardian asking him to search the bookshops for entomological books. He was himself planning to visit London in company with Kirby but the two were in dispute as to the day on which the expedition should start. The good parson wanted as many days as possible in town and suggested Simon should spend a Sunday at Barham so that they could start on a Monday. Simon had demurred, drawing the rejoinder -
"We are I trust as near Heaven at Barham as you are at Norwich".(12)

REFERENCES

1. M.H. Wilkin, op. cit. p.325
2. Wilkin Papers, 24. S.W. to J.K. January 1810
3. C.L. Brightwell, *Thomas Brightwell*, p.26
4. Norfolk Chronicle, 21 April and 5 May 1810
5. C.L. Brightwell, op. cit. pp.26 and 27
6. Wilkin Papers, 25. S.W. to J.K. 25 April 1810
7. Wilkin Papers, 27. S.W. to J.K. undated
8. Wilkin Papers, 28. S.W. to J.K. 25 June 1810
9. Wilkin Papers, 31. S.W. to J.K. 29 July 1810

10. Wilkin Papers, 29. S.W. to J.K. 16 July 1810
11. Wilkin Papers, 33. S.W. to J.K. 25 September 1810
12. C.B.J. Notes, 10. S.W. to J.K. 15 December 1810

BAPTISTS, CHAPEL. ST MARY'S.
ERECTED 1812.

Coming of age

Simon was closely involved with his guardian in the life of the church at St Mary's. The Meeting House in which they worshiped dated from about 1745 and had probably been made by gutting out an existing house. This had later been enlarged, resulting in a hall disproportionately long for its breadth, seating a congregation of about 500. Now, after some twenty years of Joseph Kinghorn's ministry, its rebuilding was mooted. Forty years later Simon told how he had discussed the plan with Thomas Hawkins, the leading deacon of the church:

"The front of the original meeting-house was built of bricks and flints mixed together (as of old was the fashion in Norwich). Standing in front to survey it we agreed that it would not do to rebuild with such old-fashioned mixture of bricks and flint; ..... Plan after plan, however, succeeded till renovated 'St Mary's' became what it is; standing back many feet from the street, with handsome iron pallisades and gates, its imposing front of white bricks with Grecian portico on an ample flight of stone steps - altogether both within and without one of the handsomest meeting-houses in the Kingdom, free however, I am happy to say, from all popery and popish adornments of Gothic within and Gothic without, as well as from all vestiges of popish canonicals!"(1)

This building which was destroyed by bombs in 1942 was designed by the Norwich architect Francis Stone and was notable for its plaster cross-vaulted ceiling. Stone also worked at the Bishop's Palace where a ceiling on the same lines can be seen in the great drawing-room.

During the building operations, which took more than a year, the people met for worship with the Congregation-alists at the Old Meeting House, Kinghorn taking the pulpit alternately with their minister, the Rev. William Hull. On March 10th 1811 Kinghorn and Simon together laid the foundation stone of the new meeting house -

"The square of the intended building was occupied by an immense mound of earth and bricks, on which the vast con-gregation was assembled as in an amphitheatre surrounding the small square area cleared (many feet below the sur-face) for the ceremony of laying the stone. There stood Mr Kinghorn's patriarchal figure, addressing the sur-rounding concourse and concluding with uplifted arms in prayer. William Taylor happened to be passing at the

moment and stopped to listen. [He] was much struck with
the whole and afterwards told me that the scene strongly
reminded him of the ceremony he witnessed at Rome on the
annual benediction of the people by the pope."(2)

In April (1811) Simon went to London again with his
brother-in-law. They took tea with Kirby en route and
spent two nights in the journey. When they arrived at the
York Hotel Simon unpacked and found no pantaloons. He
wrote to beg Nelly to send his last new pair with strings
at the ankles and steel buttons for the bracers. He was
by now an experienced traveller between Norwich and London,
a fact which was to prove useful in the emergency which
arose in the following month when alarm occasioned to the
Dissenters by the introduction of "Lord Sidmouth's Bill"
in the House of Lords. The penal provisions against nonconformists enacted after the Restoration were still
nominally in force though suspended on certain conditions
by the Toleration Act of 1689. A dissenting preacher, to
enjoy the protection of this Act, had to make a prescribed
oath and declaration and subscribe to the Thirty nine
Articles of the Church of England except for the three or
four which were the grounds of his dissent. Lord Sidmouth
sought to limit this toleration to persons recommended by
six respectable householders. His proposal aroused great
anger and apprehension among nonconformists as a move in
the wrong direction, tightening up laws they considered
long overdue for repeal. News of the alarm reached Norwich
on Saturday May 18th (1811) and immediately steps were
taken to put forward a petition to Parliament. This was
signed on the Sunday and on Monday morning - 784 signatures being obtained. Simon was now almost 21 and the
fact that he was potentially a man of means and the ward
of so eminent a divine as Joseph Kinghorn marked him out
as a leader among the dissenters of the district. He was
chosen to take their petition to London and thus recorded
his experiences:

"I proposed that Mr Kinghorn should accompany me to which
he gladly acceded. We travelled post and left ourselves
slender time for sleep on the road. In the morning when
within twenty miles of London I calculated that we should
not be able to reach our appointment at Mr Favell's
counting-house in St Mary Axe and said to Mr Kinghorn,
we must certainly take four horses for the last stage
in order to be in time, which to his great discomforture
we accordingly did, and just arrived at the hour named.
We immediately went with Mr Favell down to the House of
Lords and were introduced by William Smith (member for
Norwich) to Lord Holland. I swung out my ponderous roll
of signatures at full length along the floor and laid
the petition before his Lordship. I was struck with his
careful perusal of it, noting the principal points with
his finger and after ten minutes conversation consigned
it to his care and took our leave. As I wished to hear
the debate it was arranged that I should wait but that
Mr Kinghorn should return to Mr Favell's. Immediately
afterwards Dr Rees joined us with the same object. He
and I seated ourselves on the stairs of the house and
fell into conversation. Soon after Mr Kinghorn left us,

he returned to caution me against the night air after a
crowded house, and then again and again returned to
suggest other doubts and fears as to the probable late-
ness of the hour and difficulty of getting home. At
length on seeing him again return, I said to Dr Rees, I
must not allow Mr Kinghorn to go away alone for he will
certainly be full of anxiety for the rest of the evening
on my behalf. I then told Mr Kinghorn I should give up
the debate and rest content with reading instead of
hearing the fight. I therefore bid the Doctor farewell
and trotted off with my dear friend to his no small con-
tentment. The excitement which prevailed outside the
House was responded to within its walls. The floor was
literally covered with petitions and the peers, especially Lords Erskine and Holland were constantly to be
seen re-entering the House with fresh bundles of rolls.
The anxiety was not, however, of long duration for the
Bill was rejected ...."(3)

On July 27th 1811 Simon attained his majority. He
left his Guardian's house in Pottergate and took up residence in his late father's house at Costessey, busying
himself with alterations. He wrote to Kinghorn of his
"lively gratitude for the invariable tenderness and
affection with which you have educated me - I enjoy at
present excellent health and happiness I think almost
unalloyed. For both I have none on earth to thank but
yourself".

His principal interest and activity was still his
collection of insects. Kinghorn had gone to London to
preach for the Society for Promoting Christianity among
the Jews. Simon wrote that he was expecting a visit from
Kirby in September: would Kinghorn go to Ackerman's in the
Strand and get them to send patterns of borders for the
arrangement of the insects - a mat silvered stamped border
would be a relief to the sable monotony of his funeral
processions. Kinghorn obliged and Simon wrote that he had
chosen, childlike, the most glittering, broadest, silver
one.

Among his entomologist friends was John Curtis,
eighteen months his junior, who was engaged in uncongenial
work in the office of a lawyer in Norwich. Simon invited
Curtis to come and live at Costessey. He came and the two
formed an Entomological Society with Simon as President,
Curtis as Secretary and including in its membership the
Rev. W. Kirby, the Rev. J. Burrell, Thomas Brightwell,
Joseph Hooker, John Lindley, Joseph Sparshall and ten or
twelve others.(4)

Simon was fascinated by Latreille's system of class-
ification set out in his *Genera Crustaceorum*. He inspired
Curtis with an equal admiration of it to such an extent
that he determined to embark on the tremendous task of
describing and drawing all the genera of insects. Curtis
was an accomplished draftsman. His father, John Morgan
Curtis, had been an engraver and he now determined to learn
engraving and went to a Mr Edwards of Bungay for the purpose, dividing his time between Bungay and Costessey. He
soon mastered the craft and produced some beautiful
plates.(5) Some of these adorned *An Introduction to Entomology*

by William Kirby and William Spence, published in 1815.
In the preface the authors wrote:
"In acknowledging their obligations to their friends,
the first place is due to Simon Wilkin Esq. to whose
liberality they are indebted for the numerous plates
which illustrate and adorn the work; the whole of which
have been drawn and engraved by his artist Mr John
Curtis, whose intimate acquaintance with the subject has
enabled him to give to the figures an accuracy which
they could not have received from one less conversant
with the science."
It is not clear how long Curtis remained with Simon
but by 1817 he seems to have established himself in London.
He became one of the first people to live by practising
science. Later on (1860) he published *Farm Insects* and became a pioneer of pest control.
Besides his entomological interests Simon set up a
Botanical Garden at Costessey, purchasing the collection
of the Rev. William Jewell, the Rector of Burgh-next-
Aylsham. According to James Grigor (writing in his *Eastern
Arboretum*) Simon's friend W.J. Hooker was principally concerned with this garden and in it made 'his first essay in
the arrangement of plants under the Linnean system'. Even
when Grigor was writing, thirty years later, he says
'Though it has long run wild, some individuals may yet be
traced which formed a part of his interesting collection'.
Meanwhile the new chapel in St Mary's was going up
and the bills were coming in. While Kinghorn was still in
London, Simon wrote:
"I have done what you may blame me for but you know I am
somewhat liable to take jumps in tenebris. I have agreed
to take into my hands the whole subscription to Meeting,
to pay the Builders when covered in and give 5 pr cent
for the remnant - I am of course appointed Treasurer.
On Thursday Mr Hawkins and I went round and collected
£991.17.0 - only 2 .... declined paying the whole now.
Mr Beare gave 30£ instead of 20£. I lodged 970£ in
Gurney and took a receipt. Did I do right?"(6)
He kept an account of the subscriptions in a little
note book which was eventually lodged in the vestry at
St Mary's and so destroyed by the bombs in 1942. This
revealed that Simon himself was the largest single sub-
scriber, giving in all £800. Thomas Brightwell gave £350;
Thomas Hawkins £247.10.0. Thomas Theobald, a rising manufacturer of Norwich stuffs gave £105, his brother-in-law
Jeremiah Colman £50, while members of the Culley family
subscribed largely, their gifts totaling nearly £900.
John Crome, another member of the congregation, gave £15,
perhaps the price of a masterpiece. The building ultimately cost £3,650.
That September (1811) Joseph Kinghorn and his ward
were concerned in the formation of a Norwich branch of the
British and Foreign Bible Society, an occasion notable as
the first on which a Bishop of Norwich appeared on the same
platform with Dissenting Ministers. J.J. Gurney who had
arranged the business noted that Kinghorn seconded the vote
of thanks to the Bishop with some excellent remarks about
his liberality. The Bishop replying said some fine things

about Kinghorn.

"The Bishop's heart seemed quite full and primitive
Kinghorn, when the Bishop spoke of him so warmly, seemed
ready to sink into the earth with surprise and terrified
modesty."(7)

£700 was collected at the meeting, Kinghorn sub-
scribing ten guineas and Simon thirty. Both became
members of the local committee.

Besides his hobbies and church interests Simon was
concerned to increase his fortune. To this end Kinghorn
introduced him to Richard Fishwick in whose Elswick Lead
Works at Newcastle he had himself worked before going to
college. Fishwick had ceased his Elswick connection in
1799 but had other irons in the fire. In October 1811
Simon went to London to meet him, arriving at 7 one evening
and putting up at the White Hart in Abchurch Lane. Fishwick came in at 9 o'clock next morning. They breakfasted,
talked business till noon, then walked out to see the
ground on which it was proposed to build a factory - near
Great Surrey St in the Borough. Thence they walked to
Islington and dined at a Tavern, Mrs Fishwick and the
children being away in the North. At Park St they inspected Fishwick's museum. The exhibits included a Mermaid
  "huge shapeless ears, fingers unfurnished with bones,
  fins and tail like those of a fish".

Simon could not detect any fraud. They returned to
tea at Abchurch Lane having walked about eight miles.(8)

In 1811 Simon became a member of two learned societies concerned with Natural History. On November 16th his
name was proposed to the Wernerian Natural History Society
of Edinburgh by his friend William Elford Leach, now an
undergraduate in the medical school of the university
there. He was duly admitted a non-resident member a fortnight later. This society was named after Abraham Gottlob
Werner, Professor of Minerology and the Art of Working
Mines at Freyburg, who was made an honorary member when
the Society was founded in January 1808. During the four
years up to the date of Simon's admission about forty
resident members had been enrolled and nearly double that
number of non-residents from all parts of the United Kingdom, besides a hundred foreign members, about half of them
from France and Germany and others from as far afield as
Constantinople, the United States, Mexico and Brazil,
including such famous names as Cuvier, Lamark, Latreille
and the Baron Von Humbolt. Norfolk was already represented
by Dr J.E. Smith, Thomas Marsham and Dawson Turner. Then
on December 3rd he was elected a Fellow of the Linnean
Society in London. As we shall see he was well acquainted
with Doctor - later Sir - James Edward Smith, the Norwich
naturalist who had founded the society in 1788 and was
still its president.

Nothing had come of Simon's business negotiations
with Fishwick and in 1812 he turned in another direction,
entering into a partnership with Richard Mackenzie Bacon
in a project for making paper. Bacon was fifteen years
his senior. He had been educated at Norwich School under
Dr Forster. He was head boy in 1792 and made the customary
Latin oration to the Mayor on Guild day. From an early age

he had been engaged in the Norwich Mercury, one of the two
local weekly papers, which had been acquired by his father.
Bacon was interested in the mechanics of printing. In conjunction with Bryan Donkin of Bermondsey he had patented a
machine in which the type was held in a revolving cylinder.
This invention was exhibited at Cambridge and was said to
produce beautiful print with unequalled rapidity. One of
his machines was installed in the University Press, another
exported to Russia. Bacon was indeed a man of parts and
not without experience in paper-making. When the size of
the sheets on which the Norwich Mercury was printed had
been enlarged in 1809, he wrote that the paper which was
manufactured under his own eye would he believed be found
equal to that of other Provincial Newspapers. In 1811 he
had been advertising writing paper made at Taverham. He
had been running the Taverham mill for some years in
partnership with his brother-in-law Francis Noverre and
another Norwich man, John Gilbert. They had invested
large sums in modernisation. In 1807 Taverham had been
one of the first paper-mills in the country to be supplied
with the newly patented Fourdrinier machines producing
continuous rolls of paper on a belt of wire moulds.
Apparently Noverre and Gilbert got cold feet over the
project and their partnership was dissolved in 1812 when
Simon came in to provide more capital.(9). The Taverham
mill, when Bacon and Wilkin had vacated it six years later,
was described as comprising engines, presses, boiling-
house, sizing-house and drying lofts, capable of holding
600 reams of paper, with houses for the foreman and clerk
and twelve cottages for workmen.(10)
     In August 1812 Thomas Brightwell drew up articles
of partnership for Bacon and Wilkin and the new firm took
a lease of Taverham water-mill from Mrs Branthwaite for
£545 per annum. To provide his share of the capital Simon
obtained a loan of £3,000 from Gurney's until money should
come in from his estates. Norwich was fairly prosperous
at the time. The weavers of camblets had recently received
an advance of wages and the Mercury was writing cheerfully
of full employment. No doubt the partners of Bacon and
Wilkin were optimistic about the future of their undertaking.

REFERENCES

1. M.H. Wilkin, *Joseph Kinghorn of Norwich*, p.331
2. M.H. Wilkin, *Joseph Kinghorn of Norwich*, pp.333 and 334
3. M.H. Wilkin, *Joseph Kinghorn of Norwich*, p.340
4. *Proceedings of the Linnean Society*, Obituary of John
   Curtis, 1864
5. G. Ordish, *John Curtis and the Pioneering of Pest Control*,
   pp.16 and 17
6. Wilkin Papers, 40. S.W. to J.K. undated
7. J.B. Braithwaite, *Memoirs of J.J. Gurney*, Vol. I, p.66
8. Wilkin Papers, 39. S.W. to J.K. 18 October 1811
9. D. Stoker, Early History of Papermaking in Norfolk.
   Norfolk Archaeology, Vol. XVI, Pt III, p.244
10. Norwich Mercury, 14 February 1818

Simon's campaign

Whatever practical interest Simon took in paper-making when he entered into partnership with R.M. Bacon seems soon to have evaporated. In 1813, while the firm's overdraft with Gurney's climbed to nearly £5,000 he was frequently away from home. That Spring his attention was engaged with quite another matter - matrimony. It was not that he had fallen in love; rather he was anxious to do so and started energetically on a 'campaign' to find and win the right girl. On May 13th he wrote from London to tell Kinghorn that he was seeking an introduction to the Wilson family where there were a number of daughters:

"I mean to riggle (sic) into the clan of the said Wilsons - I hope to see them to-night at Mrs Siddons's Readings and if I can make anything of them I will let you know".(1)

When he did meet the Wilson girls he found them simple and amiable but was "not frappé". He then "pushed a column" to Battersea to meet the Benwell family. Mr B. he found charming, Harriet, sweet and amiable, but still he was "not frappé".

His friend Dr J.E. Smith who was paying his usual Spring visit to town, as one of the leading scientists of the day, had the entré into London society and Simon took advantage of his complaisance to take a look at the fashionable world. He wrote:

"I resolved to take a peep at the beau monde. I went to a rout at the sister of the late Marchioness of Rockingham's where I sauntered (Chapeau sous bras) for an hour among Marchionesses Duchesses Countesses and 'fashionables' of all sorts and sizes. I was charmed with the beauty and delighted with the variety and novelty; the Jewels I should not have half observed but for my companion Dr Smith. But what stuff it all is! I behaved myself very properly, was very polite, as nonsensical and garrulous as suited the occasion, twirled my cocked hat about with studied casualness, made myself in short as agreeable as possible and then laughed very heartily at the idiotism of what I had seen! - Quantum suff: tho't I of the *fashionable assemblage of beauty and brilliancy* - now let's see what sort of a being a Bishop be -- So I called on the Bishop of Winchester (to go as near the top as I could) found him very agreeable, his house crowded with works of art, his gardens fine, his

Daughters agreeable and accomplished and was very kindly
received and invited to dinner. -- And so far 'tis all
very well -- next night I went to the Concert Room at
the opera and here I was fain to gape because I could
not admire the Italian Singing of Strumpets and fools
and did not choose to *sigh* for any of the Creatures who
surrounded me tho' I certainly was in the midst of a
groupe of the most beautiful women I ever saw -- and yet
I was very much pleased with some of the musick and some
of the singing and could not but feel on the whole
satisfied. *Mais que devient tout cela?*"(2)

Early in August Simon was back in Norfolk taking a
holiday at Cromer with John Curtis. A Sunday there with
no Meeting House in range occasioned a letter:
"This is a day with bathing people of little import: it
is an old fashioned 12 hours which were much better out
of the calender. One is so dull; and tis not *right* to
walk about so much as on other days. And, to be sure
'tis tolerably amusing to see a great many folks well
dressed at Church, or it would really be almost impossible to exist; in a word in reckoning the length of their
stay I overheard some ladies saying 'You know I don't
count Sunday *for Anything*'!! .... And to say the truth I
never found a Sunday so dull on my hands before. Who
preaches at Cromer? Nobody Sir, only Mr Glover in the
afternoon at Church. (The Rev. George Glover M.A., Vicar
of Cromer was active in Norfolk whig politics.) William
will go to hear Cubitt. He is a serious good man but
'tis not to me quite agreeable to go to a little beggarly
uncomfortable damp church where only a few country folks
are to be seen; to blunder (as to standing and sitting
I mean) thro' a long service for the sake of a very long,
a very very dull and a woefully rambling sermon whose
only excellence is that it comes from the heart of a
truly pious man who aims to reach the hearts of those who
hear him. -- We came home and dined and Curtis is now
gone to Cromer Church. I thought of going too but then
I thought again.....

It has with me been for some time an undecided
question to what extent conformity of form, I may call
it, be allowable when at Church. Much of good I must
allow there is in the service of our Church. The prayers
are fine. And is there anything wrong in the responses
of the congregation. I would say even that it is
gratifying to have auricular as well as ocular testimony
of a union of worship between People and priest. And
with respect to the kneeling at Prayers it is surely a
humbler posture than standing or *lounging* . · Besides it is
the praying posture of the people in whose assembly I
have made myself one, and would they not with as much
justice complain of my nonconformity with their established mode, as I should of a man who should think fit to
sit still when I deem it indispensible to decorum that
everyone should stand?.....
Second Edition!! Curtis just returned with the news that
Mr Glover has been preaching a furious sermon against the
Dissenters from Jeroboam's making Priests of the lowest
of the people. This is excellent. He is said to have

preached an exactly contrary sermon before the
Bishop!"(3)
By the middle of the month he returned to his
'campaign', journeying to Southampton where he hoped for
an introduction to a Miss Tomkins on whom his sister fixed
great hopes for him. Here he first met the Randall family
with a large posse of girls to whom he proved himself a
most attentive beau - "'tis my trade now!" he wrote. They
had prayer before supper which he approved. When he met
Miss Tomkins he found her "a fineish person rather than
not and not uninteresting face". A week's acquaintance,
however, settled matters as far as she was concerned.

"Mary Tomkins is a most pious, sensible, well-informed
girl, I have not a doubt, but it won't do. I should
enjoy her company but never love her."

He was not too deeply disappointed and when he discovered that Thomas Adkins, minister of the Above Bar
Independent Church at Southampton, was engaged in a
similar camapaign and had been treading the same ground
as himself, the two became fast friends and turned their
attention to another matter of common interest. Young
Toussaint, a negro youth, described by Simon as "second
son of the Emperor of St Domingo" had recently been at
Southampton and was now at Chichester: --

"I and Adkins go to Chichester tomorrow to see him. I
mean to get him to Cossey -- to promote his views of a
mission to St D -- to see the African Missionary Society
about him and in short I hope to contribute my share
towards the glorious effect of carrying the Gospel to
the poor negroes of St D --."(4)

There was no "Emperor of St Domingo"; this young
man claimed to be son of Toussaint L'Ouverture, a notable
hero of slave-liberation, whose contribution to the history of his time is too easily passed over. It is, then,
necessary to digress in order to tell the essential out-
line of his story. Back in 1791 a move by the French
National Assembly to grant civic rights to the mullatoes
-- half-castes -- of St Domingo had set the white
colonists against the government. The latter engineered
a withdrawal of the slaves from the plantations to the
mountains. The exercise got out of hand and resulted in
an orgy of destruction in which 2000 whites and many more
negros were slain. In the course of these disorders
Toussaint emerged as leader and organiser of the slaves.
He proved an efficient general, endearing himself to his
men by sharing their hardships. His aim was liberty for
all the slaves. After effecting the defeat of a British
invasion of the island -- for the British intended to
restore slavery -- Toussaint offered himself to the French
authorities for the service of the Republic and was
appointed Lieutenant Governor. He ruled his territories
with moderation, setting his face against acts of ven-
geance and protecting equally blacks from whites and
whites from blacks. He not only drove out the British
but defeated the Spaniards, bringing the Spanish part of
the island under his rule. In 1801 he proclaimed a new
constitution which amounted to a declaration of independence. He was now, practically speaking absolute ruler

of the whole of St Domingo with an army and yearly revenue
greater than those of any European power of the second
rank.

Napoleon was altogether opposed to black power in
the Carribean and was determined to restore slavery. He
had fitted out the greatest overseas expedition hitherto
mounted, which arrived off St Domingo in 1802 under the
command of his brother-in-law Le Clerk. Toussaint and his
family were kidnapped and transported to France where he
was incarcerated in a fortress in the Jura. He died there
in the following year. Apart from eliminating Toussaint
from the scene the expedition was a total failure; war and
disease cost the lives of 63,000 Frenchmen and perhaps
double that number of negroes. Wordsworth wrote a sonnet
in honour of Toussaint but his memory was almost extinguished by the shadow of the great tyrant who had
destroyed him and still threatened Europe.(5)

Young Toussaint's affairs continued to occupy
Simon's mind over the next two years and we shall have
occasion to return to him later.

That winter the weather was adverse to trade. In
January (1814) the thermometer was 20° below freezing, the
rivers frozen hard and the roads impassable. By February
Bacon and Wilkin's overdraft exceeded £5,000. Simon was
unwell and wrote to ask Kinghorn to be present at an
interview between Bacon and J.J. Gurney on the matter.
Bacon also wrote to Kinghorn and negotiations seem to have
been left in his hands. Gurney asked for security for the
account and to have it reduced to £1,500 within three
months. Simon wrote on March 1st that he would agree to
these terms provided he could have six months instead of
three to effect the reduction. The Costessey properties
were mortgaged to the bank and for the time being anxieties
were allayed.(6)

Events in the Spring of 1814 brought Simon Wilkin
into the Norwich political arena in a role he cannot have
relished. Napoleon had been sent to Elba; General Money
a noted Norwich character who had served in the army of
Louis XVI had gone to France to accompany the King back to
Paris. The price of corn fell with the return of peace
and, as the Corporation Assembly asserted in a petition
to Parliament,

"the lower orders are now receiving considerable comfort
by being able to purchase the great staff of life on
reasonable terms".

The 'lower orders' who were accustomed to hunger and
deprivation, were determined to hold on to this comfort but
it was gained at the expense of the farmer who produced the
corn. So instead of the usual political division between
whig and tory there opened a new alignment of town versus
country. Simon, having inherited his father's mill at
Costessey, found himself on the country side of the
division. When the Norfolk millers met to consider their
interests and the propriety of a petition to Parliament
to protect the price of corn, they voted Simon into the
chair. The mere holding of such a meeting provoked a
violent reaction in Norwich. Anonymous hand bills accused
the millers of "pinching the half-filled bellies of the

pitiable poor", "fattening the already too fat landholder"
and "sacrificing the welfare of millions". Simon, as
Chairman of the millers and Thomas William Coke, as the
representative land-owner, became the immediate objects
of the indignation of the mob. They were hung in effigy
side by side in Heigham and St Benedict's and subsequently
'underwent the martyrdom by fire and faggot'.
        Simon was away at the time of this happening. His
friend R.M. Bacon supported him in the Norwich Mercury as
a gentleman 'who has never yet abandoned his conscience
for his interests' and when he returned he wrote a long
defence of his views which was published as a handbill.
Masters and men, he held, work for profit and pay -- take
away this pay and profit and no one would work. Arising
from the long wars the English farmer has to pay high
rents and taxes unlike the French who have lived on
plunder and robbery. Consequently the English farmer
cannot sell his corn as cheaply as that of foreign nations
is sold. If the foreigner sells so cheap that the English
farmer cannot pay his rent, taxes and wages he must be
ruined and the poor will lose their employ. How would
Norwich weavers get paid if foreign weavers were allowed
to come and sell cottons, camblets and shawls at half
price? In a few years on this plan no corn would be grown
in England. They would be at the mercy of foreign farmers
and millers who could starve them. Could England be
independent or flourishing if she could not feed herself?
As leases ran off land would fall and the English farmer
would in time be able to sell as low as the foreigner.
England growing her own bread and using her own manufactures and having fought for and obtained her independence
would still as before defy the world.(7)
        At a Common Hall on June 1st Simon's arguments were
answered by William Firth, Sergeant at Law, formerly
Steward of Norwich and for a time Attorney General of
Upper Canada, who said that if our farmers grew no corn we
could buy at half the price from abroad and the land might
be cultivated for pasturage so that the price of meat would
be reduced. The Common Hall was unanimous in the opinion
that the protection of corn was fraught with the most
alarming evil. As the price of labour must be proportion-
ate to the price of subsistence the increased price of
Norwich manufactures must give foreign manufacturers a
decided advantage.
        The Corn Bill was at this juncture thrown out by
Parliament and its defeat was hailed with bonfires in
Norwich.
        The matter was soon forgotten in celebrations of
the peace. The city was illuminated with a blaze of lights
and at Costessey Simon entertained nearly 250 men, women
and children in his service. They sat down to dine at six
tables laid in the orchard and finished the day's pleasures
by a rustic ball in a barn fitted up for the purpose.(8)
        At this stage in his career Simon was well endowed
with this world's goods and was disposed to use his wealth
generously. Early in 1814 he had given £100 to the Rev.
Mark Wilks for his new chapel then building in St Clements.
In August of the same year he wrote to Joseph Kinghorn,

who after his ward had left him had moved to a house in
St Faith's Lane, telling him that their old residence in
Pottergate was to be sold. He had instructed his brother-
in-law to buy it and wished to lay the deeds on his table
"You cannot but accept what you know affords me genuine
pleasure to offer -- and we shall mutually regard the
offer and the acceptance as pledges of our affection
which early began and can never be repressed between
us".(9)
    The gift was accepted with expressions of thanks
and affection.
    That autumn (1814) Simon came to a determination
that he was in need of further education. Dr Samuel
Forster, after giving up his not very successful master-
ship of the Norwich School, had gone to live at Windsor
where he was currently coaching two sons of the Earl of
Bristol. Simon joined this party and wrote to Kinghorn
from Windsor in November, describing his journey and his
mode of life there:
"I found myself inclined to relieve my horses by driving
a pair of post horses at the last stage. These brutes
were so unmanageable that, being obliged to drive without
gloves because the rain made the reins slippery, I found
my fingers excorciated when I reached my hotel on
Saturday night. On Sunday I went to Prescot Street
[Baptist Church] where I sat down [at the Lord's Supper].
Mr Griffin is a perfectly plain man in his manners and
preaching -- and in the ministration of the ordinance.
I liked him as well as I expected. For my expectations
when from home are very seldom raised to more than
mediocrity. I spent two or three days in London, in
seeing several folks .... and reached Windsor on Wedy mg.
I immediately wrote a note to Dr Forster who when I
called received me very kindly. We talked over pre-
liminaries and then I went to take possession of my
lodgings. They are very small but near Dr Forster's
and large enough to contain me and my books. I took a
walk to reconnoitre and to provide myself with paper,
pens &c &c and at four dined with the Doctor. At 11 on
Thursday we attacked Aeschylus together. Having read no
Greek for four years I was surprised at the facility with
which I found the power of reading it return ....
Before 11 I prepare Greek which we read together till
about 1 or ½ past. We then frequently walk or ride for
an hour or two. At 4 we dine. Our party is a small one
but very pleasant -- the Dr, Miss Forster, Miss Guerimand
and the Earl of Bristol's two sons, Lord Harvey and the
Hon. George Harvey: the first about 14 and the other 10
or 11. Lord Harvey is a sound classic and an excellent
scholar -- he is very polite and George *would* be so.
After dinner *we* boys go one to his lodgings, the others
upstairs .... I read Italian and after tea Latin unless
we are idle."
    Simon had not abandoned his 'campaign'. He says in
the same letter that he wishes and prays that the same
feeling of affection towards him that exists in two or
three individuals might be extended to one being more. He
seems to have contemplated some change in his way of living

31

speaking of the painfulness of leaving home perhaps more
permanently than ever before.
"I really found it more difficult than I apprehended --
one old servant after another coming in to take leave --
some dismissed, others to remain -- but all *unhappy* and
in their several modes expressing wishes towards me
which left the impression that I was not an object of
indifference to them. Poor old John who had heard that
morning from the surgeon that I had paid the bill for
his illness and the amputation of his arm -- came into
my study to thank me and take his leave which he did in
the forcible tho' unadorned language of natural eloquence
-- and parted with so zealous a 'God bless you Sir'
...."(10)
        Not many months were given to the renewed study of
the classics. By February (1815) Simon was in London
staying at Lavender Hill on the Wandsworth Road. Once more
Gurney's Bank was pressing for the reduction of his overdrafts, now amounting to about £2,800. He had hoped he
told Kinghorn, that the last harvest would have put
matters right but he had been disappointed. He was determined henceforth to spend with the greatest caution.(11)
He called in loans he had made and even asked Kinghorn if
he would sell stock and accommodate him on personal
security. (This Kinghorn did and paid £200 into his
account.) He and Bacon, he said, had been threatened with
arrest. No wonder he was somewhat depressed though he did
not attribute this to financial causes:
"I find going into the world is like the touch to the
snail's horn -- he retracts it and turns away. There
seems now to attend me only one source of unhappiness --
yet I feel and pray that I may continue to feel determined to go to my grave alone rather than marry a woman
who is not renewed by divine grace -- who cannot sympa-
thise ardently with me in those hopes which leave at
such immeasurable distance omnia terrestria, but we are
the children of circumstance and can do nothing ourselves".
        He was still pursuing his usual interests. He had
become a very decent Italian scholar and had been busy
with his insects, hoping to give Kinghorn's old-fashioned
library a star of the first magnitude in the form of
'Coleopterorum Brittanicorum in Museo Wilkiniano Catalogus'. And a
new plan was afoot. His concern about his finances was,
he said, because he did not choose to leave the Kingdom
without paying his debts.(12)
        Simon's proposed journey abroad related to his
interest in the negro youth Toussaint. Doubt had been cast
on Toussaint's pretended pedigree. On October 5th 1814 a
letter had appeared in the Times signed by him and addressed
to his mother. He had heard that she was in France -- "If
I had wings like an eagle I would be at your elbow now".
If she receives his letter he invites her to come over
immediately to him at Chichester. The letter in the Times
reached Mme Toussaint through the *Journal de Lot et Garonne.*
There was no personal reply but the Journal published a
notice which was repeated in the Times of November 15th.
"The Toussaint family requests us to publish that it

32

resides in the town of Agen. It consists of the widow
Toussaint, of her two sons who were educated at Paris,
and of her husband's niece who is married to the youngest
of her sons. There were two other brothers: one of them
died at Agen: the other accidentally remained in St
Domingo at the time when his family was treacherously
carried off from that island. He might then be about
27 years old. It is presumed that it is he who is now
in England."
        John Nelson Goulty, a Norfolk man in training for
the Congregational ministry, was interested in the case
and it was suggested to him that he should go to France to
investigate.(13) Finance was an obstacle to such a journey
but Goulty got into touch with Simon and they planned an
expedition together. On March 9th 1815 Simon wrote from
London to Joseph Kinghorn:
        "I am now seated at the Castle and Falcon Aldersgate S^t
waiting for my dinner having just despatched Blomfield
to Cornhill to change notes for Louis and Napoleons --
and 10 minutes ago having executed my will, which Blomfield will deliver into your hands in a week when he
comes down to Norwich .....
        I shall about 2 o'clk go to the Elephant and Castle,
get into the Brightelmstone coach and hope to arrive
there at nine. Goulty is gone on there yesterday and
today in the carriage which I intend to take over to
France and I hope to embark tomorrow morning.
        For the first time now I am about to leave my
country, and this under peculiar circumstances. I go
on a most difficult and arduous task. .... Yet I proceed,
so strongly am I impressed with the importance of its
object to those individuals who have become interested
abt it, or ultimately to Society and especially to the
cause of truth and religion.
        We go straight to Paris and shall use tho' with
great caution the introduction we have to the Abbe
Gregoire. If we make out a sufficiently strong case we
proceed to Agur (sic, but he surely means Agen) a journey
of near 600 miles.
        At my request Mr Hughes spent the evg. with us and
before we parted he committed us, our friend and his
cause to the Divine Protection in an admirable prayer.
Let us have yours too. We go to a strange land where
they do not worship the Lord our God and I deeply feel
my need of preserving Grace. We go there on a question
demanding wisdom and persuasion and the wisdom which is
from above."(14)
        The Abbe Gregoire, to whom Simon carried an intro-
duction, had been a significant figure in the Toussaint
story. In 1791 in the National Assembly it had been he
who moved the fateful resolutation giving civic rights to
the mulattoes of St Domingo. He had correspondence with
Toussaint, who was a devout Catholic, and succeeded in
arranging the free passage of twelve priests to St Domingo
in the face of opposition from atheists in the Directory.
A leading member of the 'Amis des Noires' he was still in
contact with St Domingo. 'Mr Hughes" was the Rev. Joseph
Hughes, Baptist Minister at Battersea, who was also founder

and secretary of the British and Foreign Bible Society.

It seems that Simon's expedition reached France safely for in a note which he wrote years later for his edition of Sir Thomas Browne's Works he recounted an incident which can only refer to this occasion. The note reads:

"I remember an amusing illustration of the addage that one man's food is another's poison in an incident of which I was witness. Some years ago visiting France in company with a Scotch gentleman, we sat down to dinner, just after landing, at a table d'hôte at Dieppe. Among the dishes which had been provided to suit the nationality of British visitors was some 'ros-bif'; a lean square lump of beef roasted to the consistence of mahogany, served up with thin sour gravy. My Scotch friend, after vainly endeavouring to feed on the French dishes, was introduced to the beef. Its toughness he might have endured, but the thin sour gravy was too much! He turned to me with a face of absolute despair, exclaiming, "I'll certainly be starved in this country'"(15)

On March 11th (1815), the day after Simon's embarkation, the Times reported the return of Bonaparte from Elba. On March 20th he was to enter Paris. No doubt these events frustrated the intended expedition of which we hear no more.

While Simon was pursuing his abortive mission, the Norwich mob indulged in a formidable demonstration against the mooted Corn Laws. It was not the millers this time but only the 'landed interest' that was a target of their resentment. When Thomas William Coke and Lord Albemarle came to the cattle market they were attacked as symbols of the landed interest and had to take refuge in The Angel which stood on the site of the present Royal Arcade. While the crowd, chiefly boys and striplings, was besieging the inn, the Mayor and Sheriffs issued from the Guildhall and the Riot Act was read. Failing to get order restored, the Mayor called in the Brunswick Hussars from the Barracks who drove the mob from the market-place, whereupon they repaired to the Mayor's house in St Saviour's and broke his windows.(16)

Meanwhile Simon's financial difficulties continued to embarass him. Gurney's were not happy about his affairs and in August 1815 he somehow raised sufficient money to pay off his overdrafts with them. These difficulties seem to have spurred him to unwonted activity. He wrote in September that he had seen his Cambridge banker -- the Fosters, Bankers at Cambridge, were fellow Baptists which perhaps facilitated matters -- and had gone to London to mature arrangements made necessary by extentions of business "superinduced by our works at Taverham and our "new engagements in Cambre". Bacon had been with him in town and had left him to negotiate fiscal arrangements with a London house and the Guarantee of a first-rate American house. Having arranged these matters he proposed to himself a six weeks tour before winter, going to Windsor and thence to Henley on Thames where Goulty and Toussaint, who was at this time living with him,

were highly delighted to see him and where he stayed nearly
a week; then on via Oxford to Birmingham to see his old
schoolfellow William Hawkins, who was candidate for a
Baptist pastorate there. Simon spent a Sunday with him,
heard him preach three times, and in the evening witnessed
his farewell to the congregation.
"...he gave in his refusal to accept the call of 2/3 of
the church because of one man -- and the whole congregation so to speak were in tears at parting".
The two travelled together to Burslem where Hawkins
was to supply "a rising interest", passing through "a very
singular acherontic country" of coal pits and iron
works.(17)   He went on to Liverpool --
"The buildings are generally speaking very fine --
Exchange buildings, Town Hall, St Pauls (in imit^n of
St P. London) St Nicholas, St Thomas, the Lyceum,
Athenaeum and Union, News Rooms and Libraries, Infirmary,
Dispensary, Blue Coat Hospital, Jews Synagogues,
Independent and Baptist Chapels, besides Theatre,
Rotunda and the first Blind Ayslum in the Kingdom.   The
blind sing publicly twice a week, some fine trio,
quartette, duet and single songs."
He went thence to Chester, crossing the Mersey by
packet boat.   The passage was rough and after beating
against the wind and tide the boat gave up the general
landing place and put her passengers ashore two miles down
stream.   At Chester he was shewn the Cathedral which he
thought the poorest in the kingdom, built of red freestone
very indurable.   At Northwich he inspected a salt mine.
"I entered a tub or bucket first, dressed like a Carter
& thro' an apperture about 6 feet square descended 330
feet".
Accompanied by other visitors each carrying two
naked candles the guide took him round the vaults cut in
the salt --
"When the whole is lighted it is by reflection of the
crystals very splendid -- The general colour is red-
brown veined with a pure white crystal".
He visited Lord Grosvenor's Eaton Hall, the finest
modern Gothic mansion, he thought, in the country, slept
at Tern Hill, breakfasted at Shrewsbury and reached
Worcester on Saturday night October 31st.   Here he had
intended pursuing his 'campaign', but his hopes were
slight:
"What am I about?   Did I not set out with a determination
to succeed?   Was I not guilty of attempting to snatch
from Providence the reins & say I will delay no longer?"
He had a presentiment that the object of his visit
to Worcester would altogether fail, and it did.   Despite
this he wrote that he had been very much delighted with
his tour.(18)

REFERENCES

1. C.B.J. Notes 13. S.W. to J.K. 14 May 1813
2. Wilkin Papers, 49. S.W. to J.K. undated
3. Wilkin Papers, 45. S.W. to J.K. 5 August 1813

4. Wilkin Papers, 60. S.W. to J.K. undated
5. R. Korngold, *Citizen Toussaint*, London 1945
6. C.B.J. Notes 15 and 17. S.W. to J.K. 7 February and
   1 March 1814.
   C.B.J. Notes 16. R.M.B. to J.K. 12 February 1814
   H.E. Gunton, *Chronological Costessey*, Vol. I, Pt 2, p.59
7. Norwich Mercury, 21 May 1814
8. Norwich Mercury, 18 June 1814
9. Wilkin Papers, 50. S.W. to J.K. undated
10. Wilkin Papers, 51. S.W. to J.K. November 1814
11. C.B.J. Notes 18. S.W. to J.K. 3 February 1815
12. Wilkin Papers, 55. S.W. to J.K. 7 February 1815
13. H. Crabb, Robinson Papers, 1149. Goulty to
    Mr and Mrs Pattison, 17 November 1814
14. Wilkin Papers, 56. S.W. to J.K. 9 March 1815
15. *Sir Thomas Browne's Works*, Bohn 1852, Vol. I, p.352
16. Norfolk Chronicle, 18 and 25 March 1815
17. Wilkin Papers, 62. S.W. to J.K. 27 September 1815
18. Wilkin Papers, 64. S.W. to J.K. 25 and 28 October 1815

Sorrow and loss

Simon enjoyed a very close relationship with his sister Mary, Mrs Brightwell. The fact that they had been doubly orphaned had made them the more dependent on one another. It was therefore a heavy blow to him when she died a month after the birth of her third son on November 6th 1815. Mary was strong in her faith. Her daughter recorded:

"Her end was peace: shortly before she breathed her last, her beloved pastor Mr Kinghorn having said, 'Shall we pray?' she replied, 'Yes and praise too'."(1)

Simon had not expected her death. He wrote:

"The bereavement which an allwise providence has inflicted came upon me unawares -- and still it seems to me a dream ..... I have at length lost my other self, that being with whom I shared the delights of infantine happiness and with whom I have ever since divided the successive joys and sorrows of life even to the hour of her Death. ... Now all that remains is to be thankful and resigned -- Thankful for the calm tranquility and happiness with which my dear sister expired and resigned to the will of that Being who called her to himself."

He turned for comfort to his old guardian:

"Every fresh instance of my distress -- or difficulty -- brings with it a fresh instance of your kindness."(2)

More distress and difficulty was to follow on the heels of Simon's bereavement. The victory at Waterloo had been celebrated that summer with bonfires and bell-ringing but the ensuing peace had not brought prosperity. A post-war slump set in with a high degree of unemployment aggravated by demobilisation. There was great distress among the poor. In May 1816 a hungry mob assembled in Norwich marketplace and moved to the New Mills where they broke in and pillaged. The following October John Pitchford speaking at a Common Hall called to discuss the prevailing distress thus described the situation:

"Agriculture, manufactures and commerce all unnaturally strained by the war are now staggering and reeling under a depression as unexampled as was their former unnatural elevation".(3)

The Taverham enterprise was adversely affected by the slump. Probably an attempt had been made at a substantial expansion of its activities just at the time when the economy was moving into a recession. Despite all

efforts by the partners money was not forthcoming to
pay the bills of Bacon and Wilkin or to meet Simon's
personal liabilities. In July 1816 he asked Thomas
Brightwell to join him in a personal security to his
bankers and was much put out when his brother-in-law
refused to do so.(4) His partner Bacon informed Kinghorn
that Simon owed no less than £10,850 and wrote six sides
of foolscap on plans to avoid a bankruptcy. Whatever
scheme was to be adopted he considered Kinghorn's advocacy
indispensible. William Unthank, his lawyer. recommended
bankruptcy as the only means of emancipating him from his
private engagements.(5) Pressure came from the London
creditors. Simon wrote that the danger of himself or
Bacon going to town would be great as to arrest. He was
prepared to offer the London creditors if they would let
him go on trading that he would pay all eventually or if
they preferred a composition they should hear what his
friends would guarantee.(6) In a mood of pessimism he
wrote:

"If we are not enabled to keep Taverham, I prophesy that
my friends will let me sink gradually into nothing. I
shall either be obliged to take a clerk's place at £50
per annum or to become an adventurer -- I fear I have
no friends".(7)

R.M. Bacon and S. Wilkin, Paper Manufacturers of
Taverham, were made bankrupt on August 29th 1816 and Simon
Wilkin, Miller of Costessey, on September 2nd. A valuation
was made of Paper, Rags &c at Taverham and Costessey --
they were worth £4,841.15.6.

News of Simon's insolvency brought a claim from a
forgotten creditor. Henry Hobbs of Chichester wrote to
Kinghorn that he had spent £50 on maintaining a black
youth, son of General Toussaint, placed under his care at
Wilkin's request who had promised to pay his board. Simon
had asked him if he could make it convenient to take the
young negro until an opportunity offered of getting him
back to St Domingo. Prince Sanders had written to
Toussaint saying that he wanted to go to St Domingo and
would be happy to have him as a companion. (Sanders, a
black American, then in London, was going as an envoy from
Wilberforce to King Henry Christophe who was then ruling
the North part of the island.) On receipt of this letter
Hobbs had applied to Goulty for directions. After a long
delay Goulty had informed him that Simon intended to do
no more for the youth than to see Hobbs paid. Hobbs
understood that Goulty had been paid in full for costs
incurred relating to Toussaint. Ought not the sum to be
divided between them? He was willing to leave matters to
the judgement of Kinghorn and Brightwell.(8) The reason
for Simon's withdrawal of his support from Toussaint was
probably his own financial embarrassment but he may also
have concluded that the youth was an imposter.

Simon suffered a further humiliation in that Kinghorn advised him to stay away from the observance of the
Lord's Supper at St Mary's. A bankruptcy might be evidence
of moral lapse if the negligence or extravagance of the
bankrupt had contributed to the losses of his creditors
and, as Kinghorn said, "the minds of some have been much

hurt". Simon felt this stigma deeply and for some weeks stayed away from the church altogether until he wrote that he could not bear to be excluded longer.

A meeting of creditors was held at the White Swan in St Peter's on November 16th 1816 to decide what was to be done with the mill and farms at Costessey at present let to John Culley of Ringland. Three days later at 10 am on Tuesday November 19th the curious and interested met at Costessey for the sale of Simon's effects. 227 lots of books were sold that day - 58 lots of Theology, 28 of Dictionaries and Lexicons, 70 of Voyages, History etc. including such diverse items as Godwin's Political Justice, Winterbotham's America and Blomefield's Norfolk, 6 lots of Greek and Hebrew Bibles and 65 of books in Latin, French and Italian. The next day were sold 35 lots of Poetry and 135 of Natural History including Kirby and Spence's *Introduction to Entomology* with its superbly engraved illustrations provided by Curtis at Simon's expense. Nothing was held back. Even the four volumes of Latreille's *Genera Insectorum* which had been Simon's constant guide and companion for so long came under the hammer. The third day the auctioneers disposed of 122 lots of miscellaneous books including Malthus on the *Principles of Population* and Adam Smith's *Wealth of Nations*. Then followed 39 lots of Engravings and Drawings including 13 watercolours by John Sell Cotman and a folio of Curtis's coloured drawings of insects and 6 of his copperplates. There were 33 lots of Shells, Silver and Copper Coins and other oddments but most important of all the great Collection of Insects which had been their owner's main interest for the past five years and were to have been the subject of the *Coleopterorum Britanniarum in Museo Wilkiniano Catalogus* . The collection which was divided into 16 lots comprised 10,000 specimens of 5,000 distinct species arranged after the system of Latreille. The British Museum sent down a Mr Stevens to bid for them but he was not authorised to spend more than £250 and so the collection was lost.(9) It was ultimately acquired by the Zoological Society.

So Simon parted with his most cherished possessions. It was six months later when the auctioneers were ready to deal with his properties. At 3 pm on Saturday May 10th 1817 at the Rampant Horse Inn in St Stephen's, Messrs Basham and Harman offered

"all those Water Corn Mills and Premises at Costessey in excellent repair and in which a most extensive trade has been carried on for many years by Mr Wilkin, with about 20 acres of land. .... These mills are situate on a fine stream of water, are now capable of manufacturing at least 25 lasts a week and can be made to do nearly as much more".

Besides the mills there were a 94 acre farm at Costessey and a farm of 290 acres across the river, known as Drayton Lodge.

"The country is picturesque with fine situations for building and the property altogether possesses many advantages to any person desirous of making an investment."(10)

The water mill and lands were purchased for £13,000

by John Culley,(11) a fellow member of St Mary's Baptist Church, who was to become Simon's father-in-law some years later.

Simon's partner R.M. Bacon was also bankrupt and the auctioneers selling the Costessey properties, on the same occasion offered:

"A very desirable freehold estate situate in Little Cockey Lane, Norwich, consisting of an old-established shop in full trade .... together with certain warehouses used as printing rooms, formerly in the occupation of Mr Bacon, the printer and editor of the Norwich Mercury...."

This property was acquired by Bacon's father-in-law Burks who employed him to edit the Norwich Mercury. When Burks died in 1826 Bacon once more became the proprietor.

It now became imperative to find a means of livelihood for Simon. In consultation with Joseph Kinghorn he determined on printing and publishing and the two of them began to seek a suitable opening. There were at this time several printers established in Norwich. The most active were the publishers of the two local papers, Burks and Kinnebtook of the Norwich Mercury and Stevenson and Matchett of the Norfolk Chronicle. There were at least five other small presses operating but Simon and his advisors evidently considered that there was room for yet another. In September 1817 Simon, staying at Wisbech, wrote to Kinghorn of the relative advantages of a partnership with 'K' or 'Y'. Who 'K' was is not apparent - Simon thought him ignorant of book-binding, printing and publishing and incompetent in bookselling. 'Y' was William Youngman, who in his early days had been a fellow-lodger with Kinghorn at Mrs David's and was now established as a Wine Merchant. He had kinsmen who were printers at Witham in Essex. Simon thought he would be a real help in the conduct of business and that the advantage of the Witham connection would be considerable. He, Simon, intended to acquire the necessary technical knowledge of printing and publishing. He hoped that if Youngman put in £1,000 and if he could provide £1,500 or £2,000 and devote all his time to the business he might take two thirds of the profits. But he must leave the choice of 'K' or 'Y' to the friends who were prepared to help him with the provision of capital.(12) His friends chose Youngman and Simon went to Witham to learn the trade from his prospective partner's kinsman Philip Youngman who had his press at Maldon four miles away. He wrote that he was very comfortable there, very hard at work and getting on as well as he had hoped. He thought he could find at least £1,000 from the wreck of his estates towards his capital. His friends had met at his brother Brightwell's and there were eight promises to subscribe £100 each - J[oseph] G[urney], J.J.G[urney], J. Culley, S. Culley, T. Brightwell, Richard Dawbarn and his lawyers, Foster and Unthank. Possibly Thomas Bignold Junior and other St Mary's friends would help and some might be willing to go to £150.(13)

Simon evidently worked hard and soon mastered his chosen trade. Suitable premises were obtained at No. 2

Gentleman's Walk, a shop which had previously been kept by Nathaniel Bolingbroke, silversmith and haberdasher.

With the troubles attending his bankruptcy Simon had been unable to pursue his 'campaign' in search for a bride. His emotions must surely have been stirred when in October (1817) he read in the paper of the marriage of his one-time friend Caroline Hollick to one Joseph Tickell of Hackney.

REFERENCES

1. *Memorials of the Life of Thomas Brightwell of Norwich*, p.35
2. Kinghorn Letters, S.W. to J.K. December 1815
3. Norwich Mercury, 19 October 1816
4. C.B.J. Notes 24. S.W. to J.K. 6 July 1816
5. C.B.J. Notes 32. R.M.B. to J.K. undated
6. C.B.J. Notes 33. S.W. to J.K. undated .
7. C.B.J. Notes 35. S.W. to J.K. undated
8. Wilkin Papers, 70. H. Hobbs to J.K. 1 November 1816
9. M. Allen, *The Hookers of Kew*, p.72
10. Norwich Mercury, 10 May 1817
11. H.E. Gunton, *Chronological Costessey*, Vol. X, Pt 2, p.74
12. C.B.J. Notes 36. S.W. to J.K. 18 September 1817
13. C.B.J. Notes 37. S.W. to J.K. undated

Shopkeeper

In February 1818 Wilkin and Youngman advertised
that they had started business at No. 2 Gentlemen's Walk,
a shop looking across the marketplace to the Guildhall.
Their business comprised bookselling, printing, binding
and the supply of stationery. Besides these they offered
other items which might catch the public interest. In
March they were advertising Vegetable Bitters, a cheap and
wholesome substitute for hops, and in June Dr Brewster's
patent Kaleidoscope which, the Mercury reported, was all
the rage in the metropolis. A kaleidoscope acquired by
Seth Stevenson, proprietor of the Norfolk Chronicle, had
been studied at a meeting of the United Friars' Society
in April 1818 and was described in their records as 'an
ingenious philosophical instrument, the invention of Dr
Brewster of Edinburgh, of the most simple construction
but capable of effecting an endless variety of optical
illusions'. Probably Simon's interest in the kaleidoscope
arose from the United Friars' proceedings. His neighbour,
Thomas Eaton, was an active member of the society and a
little later on he was himself to become involved with
them.
Printing orders began to come in. The earliest that
has been traced came from the Court of Guardians of the
Poor. Suspecting that they were paying out more than was
necessary, they decided to publish lists of all those
receiving out-door relief on Ladyday 1818 and invited
employers to notify them of the earnings of employees
belonging to the families listed. The lists for Conisford
and the North wards were printed by Wilkin and Youngman.
Another commission came from the Norwich Union Insurance
Societies. Complaints about the Societies' management had
resulted in meetings being held in London at which the
founder of the business, Thomas Bignold senior, had been
ousted from his position as Secretary in favour of his son
Samuel. A lengthy account of the proceedings was published in London and an abbreviated version was entrusted
to Wilkin and Youngman to meet the local demand for
information. As might be expected the firm had its share
of the sermons and addresses so numerously printed at the
time; among them John Alexander's oration at the laying of
the foundation-stone of Princes Street Chapel in 1819, and
in 1820 the Old Meeting minister's discourse on the duty
of Christians to Civil Rulers, preached on the accession

of George IV to the throne. Nor did Simon's naturalist
friends forget him - in June 1819 William Jackson Hooker
was writing to him about a publication and the cost of
colouring plates for it.
Times were now more prosperous in Norwich. In the
elections for the Common Council in March 1818 - in which
the Blue and White party triumphed - so much money changed
hands that the Norwich Mercury recommended the poor
fellows who had received £10, £15, £20, £30 or even more
for their franchise to place the money in the newly established Savings Bank lest they be tempted to make their
abundance the means of severer want. In April the
Bombazine trade was reported flourishing; in August
Camlets more flourishing then ever remembered. Houses
were being built outside the city walls near Ber Street
Gates, Chapel Field and Bull Close. But set against this
measure of prosperity was an apprehension that much was
wrong with the state of the nation. Reviewing the situation in January 1819 R.M. Bacon wrote of the dangerous
relaxation of public morals, the pestilent activities of
the desperate though small party of revolutionists, the
chaotic state of the national finances, the emigration of
capital and talent, murders dreadfully frequent, theft
matured into a profession and wives and children forsaken
for the sake of excesses to be bought at the gin shop.
In February Bacon was lamenting the incompetence of
politicians, content to prop an empire as it tottered on
the brink of ruin. In August concern for the state of the
nation was focused on the disturbances at Manchester - the
Peterloo massacre. On August 21st 1819 - only two days
after the occurrence - the Norwich papers reported a
tumult and the death of a special constable. The rest of
the story gradually filtered through - the charge of the
Yeomanry on an unarmed crowd causing death and injury to
women and children. A week or so later when the Norwich
freemen elected Edward Taylor to be Sheriff he spoke of
the late dreadful and bloody scene enacted at Manchester -
"We have seen the laws of our country violated not by
what is usually and contemptuously called the mob, but
by the magistrates themselves, aiding abetting and
instigating a wanton and unprovoked breach of peace.
Men, women and children, unarmed and unprotected have
been savagely butchered...."(1)
A number of whig supporters requisitioned a Common
Hall to discuss the Manchester transactions. This was
duly called on September 16th when the Mayor, Nathaniel
Bolingbroke, took the chair. The meeting which was solely
supported by the blue-and-whites agreed on an address to
the Prince Regent asserting the right of public assembly
and calling for an inquest into the cruel conduct of the
Manchester Magistrates. It was also agreed to raise a
subscription in aid of the Manchester sufferers -- a subscription which proved remarkable for the number of small
gifts of 1d, 2d or 3d; indeed the bulk of the 2,700
subscribers gave 6d each or less. Orange and purple
supporters largely boycotted the meeting, a fact which
enabled the whigs to make the following imputation:
"Shrinking from manly and open discussion of a great

constitutional question the advocates of Manchester Law
assembled to the amount of a dozen in some private room
and thence issued what they called a Declaration...."(2)
The Declaration lamented the riotous practices of
the seditious and disaffected and generally supported the
authorities in aid of the security and welfare of the
Kingdom. No doubt Simon was too busy with his own affairs
to take any part in these demonstrations, but we can be
tolerably sure he would have been with his fellow dissenters on the whig side. Curiously, his former protégé
John Curtis was one of the signatories to the Declaration.
The work of Simon's new press was competent and the
business was evidently successful for by January 1821 he
was able to stand on his own feet and his partnership with
William Youngman was dissolved. In his first year he
printed another document for the Norwich Union, a funeral
sermon, and 'A Defence of the Baptists' by George Gibbs
of St Clement's Chapel. An advertisement in March 1822
gives some account of his business. He was offering a
large assortment of such Juvenile Works as might safely be
placed in the hands of the young either for instruction or
amusement - mainly works of travel and discovery. He had
a stock of the best ornamental stationery including
drawing paper and borders and had just received a selec-
tion of the most approved patent medicines.
Simon does not appear to have indulged in undue
self-pity on the change of his circumstances. He took
pleasure in his newly acquired skills and opportunities
as a printer and publisher. Some of his fellow shopkeepers as well as commercial and professional men were
members of the United Friars Society which had been
founded in 1785 to emulate the monks and friars of the
middle ages in their scientific interests, love of
learning and philanthropy, while disclaiming their religious functions and substituting decent mirth for their
rules of austerity. Every member was assigned to some
order of monks or friars and on formal occasions wore the
appropriate robes. In October 1821 Simon was introduced
to the Society by Richard Taylor, a Land Surveyor by
profession and a geologist and antiquary. Taylor had
recently published his *Index Monasticus*, a study of the
religious foundations in the ancient Kingdom of East
Anglia. He had proudly read to the Society a letter from
Sir Walter Scott, 'the great Poet and Antiquary of the
North' commending his Index - 'Without such a work the
study of History is a labyrinth without a clue'. On
October 23rd Simon Wilkin and another novice were introduced and professed. The reigning Abbot, Richard Morgan,
the Norwich Union Actuary, delivered the charge pointing
out the usefulness of knowledge and scientific research.
The novices were conducted to their seats at the Table and
the Grace Cup circulated to their healths. Simon was
appointed to the order of Austin Friars. Among those
present that evening were three of his fellow shopkeepers,
Thomas Eaton, silk-mercer, his neighbour on the Walk,
J. Bennett, locksmith and clock-maker in Briggs' Lane and
J.F. Priest, chemist and druggist in St Giles's. The
first two were tories and Churchmen, of the opposite

44

persuasion to Simon in politics and religion, but the United Friars had at all times included men of varying opinion. Two days after Simon's profession the Society met again for the annual appointment of officers. Thomas Martineau, a surgeon, brother of James and Harriet, should have taken over the Abbacy but he pleaded ill health and Richard Morgan was continued for another year. Simon was appointed Procurator with the duty of keeping the minutes of the Society's transactions. The brethren that night discussed the proposed alterations on the Castle Hill with a view to erecting a new County Gaol and found themselves unanimously opposed to them. The new buildings, they thought, would ill resort together with the old Castle and they feared the loss of the beautiful panoramic walk round the Hill which contributed to the ornament of the city as well as the pleasure and health of its inhabitants. On November 6th they discussed the policy or impolicy of colonisation. The Abbot argued that without the colonies commercial relations with other countries would have been as extensive as they in fact were, an opinion not shared by the rest. They also enjoyed a cake, made and donated by a 'fair nun'.

In the new year (1822) the Society discussed Agriculture and the distresses of the Agricultural Classes. A County Meeting a few days later was to debate this subject and send a petition to Parliament calling for lower taxation and the restoration of money values. The Friars were inclined to blame the low price of corn. Later in the month they conversed upon the produce of labour and rates of wages. The Procurator often summed up their transactions as 'general conversation' and when they met on January 22nd Richard Taylor proposed that he should be asked to illustrate the term. Simon took up the task with gusto and wrote three full pages which may be summarised as follows:

Circulation of the blood - motions of heavenly bodies - the present state of the weather - the philosophy and construction of barometers - the nature of Gas light and flame - the means of preventing accidental death - Irish thrift and Irish potatoes - roasting potatoes, grilling chickens and devilling turkeys - Christmas turkeys and suits instituted against coach proprietors for fatal delays in the delivery of them - the abundance of reindeer moss on Mousehold heath - Mousehold 'whose ancient state was contrasted with the modern, not without some regret on the part of brethren who reverted to its wild extent as having afforded ample scope for their rambling capacities in boyish Days' - rural places - the inexpediency of burying in churches - iron coffins - bequests in darker ages to purchase a grave among various orders of friars - King John's policy in being buried in a cowl - the trial and execution of two witches at Lowestoft in 1664 - 'Here the brethren were interrupted by the Father Prior, who after reminding them of the flight of time proceeded in regular order to close the chapter'.

No such detailed account of an evening's conversation was thereafter recorded but the Procurator noted the main theme of the meetings. In April after the

company had sung God save the King in honour of His
Majesty's birthday, Brother Eaton read a very ingenious
translation from the Latin on 'Nothing'. A week later the
Father Abbot took up the theme announcing that he should
read 'nothing' to disturb the monotony of the chapter or
tax the Procurator's brains in recording it. Simon wrote,
"The learned and ingenious Father convinced us by reading
nothing and saying less that nothing has been undervalued
and the common proverb is utterly false - that out of
nothing, nothing can arise".

In May Simon himself entertained the chapter with
particulars learned from a gentleman who had been collecting Roman urns and reliques at Caistor near Norwich for
which the brethren kindly drank his health. At the end of
May the Friars supped together on lamb before breaking up
for their summer adjournment.

That summer (1822) proved a tumultuous one in Norwich. Simon, standing at the window of his house above
the shop in Gentlemen's Walk could watch the scene in the
marketplace and feel the pulse of the city. Work had become scarce in the Weaving Trade and the Manufacturers
talked of reducing the rates of wages agreed with the
Journeymen Weavers some years earlier, a suggestion which
was strenuously resisted. The manufacturers held a
meeting in the Guildhall and agreed to receive a deputation of twelve weavers. A crowd assembled outside the
Hall, just under Simon's windows, to support the cause of
the weavers. William Bossley, a manufacturer, arriving
late for the meeting was stopped and beaten up as an
example to the others. The deputation of weavers argued
that there was no need for a reduction but frankly said
that in any case they dared not agree to one. When one of
the manufacturers who had opposed the cut came out of the
Hall the crowd carried him shoulder-high back to his warehouse - others who were thought to have supported it were
hooted and attacked. In the end the combination of in-
timidation with a lucky increase in orders resulted in the
old wage-rates being maintained for another three years or
so.

When the Friars met again in September they discussed the proposed Navigation from Lowestoft to Norwich
designed to make the city a port. They waxed enthusiastic
about the project which they thought would avoid 'the
immense plunder now existing' when goods had to be trans-
shipped at Yarmouth and 'would create an Epoch in the
History of our City'.

Though Simon's entries in the Transactions of the
United Friars shew that he entered into the spirit of their
proceedings and enjoyed their company, yet he decided that
he did not wish to prolong the association. He had a new
interest in the proposed Norfolk and Norwich Literary
Institution. He had long been a member of the Norwich
Public Library, serving on its committee as early as 1810.
The Library badly needed a larger income but attempts to
increase its rate of subscription were constantly voted
down by the majority of members. In 1820 Wilkin and Youngman had printed a pamphlet for Dr John Yelloly proposing
the formation of a reference section to the library with an

additional subscription for those who wished to use it.
Yelloly had gone into the library's finances and found
that only about half of the sum raised annually by the
12/- subscriptions was available for buying books - an
average of £164 per annum. At Hull the subscription was
25/- and £370 a year was spent on books; at Newcastle
subscribers paid a guinea a year and also contributed to
a building fund. Yelloly's ideas did not find favour.
Again at the Annual Meeting in September 1822 Edward
Taylor proposed an increase in the subscription to 15/-
per annum - the motion was lost by 41 votes to 74. The
library was clearly unable with its restricted finance to
give an adequate service to its members - further the
librarian came in for criticism: it was said that he had
overcharged forfeits to some and received 'douceurs' from
others for special treatment. A group of those who wanted
a better library service now determined on a new and
independent venture. On October 8th 1822 about fifty of
them met at the Guildhall and agreed to found the Norfolk
and Norwich Literary Institution. John Harvey who chaired
the meeting and was appointed President of the new body
was the most active and most popular of the leading
citizens. He had been Mayor as long ago as 1792, an office
held by his father and grandfather before him, and was to
be High Sheriff of Norfolk in 1825. He was credited with
introducing to the city the shawl-manufacture for which
Norwich became famous and at this very time the Journeyman
Weavers to the number of 2,361 had just completed a subscription with a view to presenting to him a silver vase
'in testimony of the high esteem with which they regard-
[ed] him as a liberal patron and spirited promoter of
the manufacturers of his native city and as a small
tribute of gratitude for the many acts of kindness he
has manifested towards them. ...'
    The meeting appointed as Vice Presidents Sir James
Edward Smith, Hudson Gurney M.P. and Charles Harvey M.P.,
the Recorder of Norwich, all Fellows of the Royal Society,
and as Librarian and Secretary Simon Wilkin. Determined
that the new venture should not suffer from the penury
that inflicted the Public Library they ordained much
higher subscriptions - those who purchased £5.5.0. shares
were to pay £1.11.6. a year, others £2.2.0. The sum of
£1,300 was realised at the initial meeting. A management
committee was appointed - it included Joseph Kinghorn,
Thomas Brightwell and Richard Morgan - and held its first
meeting at Simon's house on the Walk that very evening.
    The United Friars met on October 29th when they
recorded in their transactions:
    "Bro. Wilkin this Evening stated to the Brethren that in
consequence of his Engagements with the Norwich Literary
Institution he will be entirely prevented from attending
the duties of the College and that he feels himself
therefore under the necessity of withdrawing from the
Society. The Brethren received this Intelligence with
much concern and must ever regret the secession of a
gentleman from whose superior talents and amiable deportment they have derived much information and pleasure.
They drank to the Health and future success of Bro. Wilkin

and took leave of him as a Friar with expressions of the sincerest esteem and regard."

Simon's engagements with the Institution were indeed considerable - the committee had already met ten times during October. In December (1822) he announced that in consequence of his engagements with the Norfolk and Norwich Literary Institution he found it expedient to move to the house in the Haymarket lately occupied by Mr David, upholsterer. These commodious premises were to provide a dwelling, shop and printing works and also a Reading Room for the Institution. The move was duly effected and the Reading Room opened there on January 1st 1823 with Reviews and Magazines though the circulation of books did not start till the following May. Simon was to receive £40 a year for the rent of the Reading Room including the cost of cleaning and lighting fires, and he was to have a salary of £50 with the obligation to provide attendance from ten in the morning till nine at night on all weekdays excepting only Christmas day and Good Friday. He was to supply all books required at 10% below publication prices, any profit beyond this accruing to himself.

Despite difficulties caused by carts, carriages and wagons which were liable to interrupt access to the rooms in the Haymarket the Institution prospered and naturally caused repercussions in the old Public Library. J.W. Robberds, its President, resented the competition of what he described as an 'aristocratical institution' and complained that it was

'the least offensive of their professed objects that ours should quietly maintain its subordinate and humbler station'.(3)

Some colour was given to these complaints when at the annual meeting of the Public Library John Harvey, J.J. Gurney, Joseph Kinghorn and other prominent members of the Institution opposed the raising of the subscription to £1.1.0. on the grounds that the Library had been set up to provide cheap reading for the public. Twice as many members attended the meeting as had done in the previous year and after hearing their President speak with great eloquence for three quarters of an hour, despite the opposition, they agreed to the increase in the subscription.

The Literary Institution had hoped to get a flying start with its book collection by buying the stock of the Surry Institution. Simon went to London to inspect the books in company with Thomas Amyot, the Antiquary, but terms could not be agreed and in March 1823 the committee met on three successive evenings and worked on lists prepared by knowledgeable members, marking urgent items for prompt purchase. In the next six months £1,500 was spent. Some of the books, particularly the literary classics, came from Simon's own stock; many were bought from London booksellers; some again were picked up at local auctions -- nine works for instance at the sale of the late John Crome's effects. There were two consignments of books from Paris costing £150. There were many donations -- the Foreign Book Society gave its collection of French and Italian publications. At the Annual Meeting in October 1823 Simon was able to report that there were 4,000 books on the shelves. The two libraries were to continue to run parallel to one-another till 1886 when they joined forces as The Norfolk and Norwich Library.

While the Literary Institution was being formed for the benefit of well-to-do citizens, William Youngman and John Withers Dowson, a young lawyer with an enthusiasm for education, were promoting a library for Working People. To give this library a start thirty citizens, Simon among them, were enlisted as shareholders. Some also gave volumes; Simon, the Works of Josephus. The reading matter was strong in travels, voyages and natural history and included books on the arts, manufactures and sciences, some geography and history, moral tales and essays and a few juvenile items such as the *Swiss Family Robinson* and *Sandford and Merton*. For the use of these books members paid a penny a week. By 1824 when Simon printed a catalogue for the Penny Library it could boast about 350 volumes.

REFERENCES

1. Norwich Mercury, 4 September 1819
2. G. Wright. *A List of Subscribers to the Manchester Sufferers,* Norwich 1819
3. Norwich Mercury, 30 August 1823

Established in the Haymarket

In December 1822 Simon advertised that he had just opened his shop in the Haymarket and offered a collection of the best works in every department of literature besides writing-desks and backgammon tables and the most recent juvenile publications in elegant bindings suitable for Christmas and New Year gifts.(1) His business had developed sufficiently for him to take on **sixteen-year-old** Josiah Fletcher as an apprentice. Josiah came from Henley-on-Thames and had been educated in the intense religious atmosphere of John Bullar's school at Southampton. He had no doubt been introduced to Simon by John Nelson Goulty then minister of the Independent church at Henley. Besides living and working with his master, Josiah went to worship with him at St Mary's where he was baptised on profession of his faith by Joseph Kinghorn three years later. He was in due time to become Simon's partner and ultimately to take over the business from him and to bring his bride to inhabit the house in the Haymarket.

In the summer of 1822 when Joseph Kinghorn had made the formidable journey into Scotland to preach and collect funds on behalf of the Baptist Missionary Society, Simon sought his aid to settle a dispute with the firm of Waugh and Innes who had refused to pay his bill. The prices, he said, were fairly charged but he gave Kinghorn carte blanche to settle on the best terms he could -- "I have no notion of such fellows to deal with", he wrote. What he had supplied to such distant customers is not disclosed; possibly pamphlets of his printing.

Kinghorn's Scottish journey had another important consequence. Half a century earlier Dr James Robertson, Professor of Oriental Literature at Edinburgh, had published his *Clavis Pentateuchi*, a commentary in Latin on the Hebrew Pentateuch. Kinghorn, who was one of the foremost Hebraists of his day, proposed to bring out a revised edition of this work and it seems that on this visit he obtained the use of Robertson's own interleaved copy to work from. To this he added numerous notes and amendments employing his acquaintance with the Chaldee, Syriac and Arabic tongues as well as Hebrew.(2) The work when complete was entrusted to Simon for printing. Simon forged the necessary fount of Hebrew type and published the Clavis in 1824, an achievement which went towards justifying M.H. Wilkin's statement in the Dictionary of National

Biography that his father greatly raised the character of the Norwich Press and issued some very erudite works.

By now Simon had become sufficiently independent to take a small part in public affairs and sufficiently affluent for his name to appear occasionally in the published lists of charitable subscriptions. In April 1823 he was one of some seventy citizens who signed a requisition for a meeting to petition parliament for the abolition of Colonial Slavery. Earlier on the abolition of the slave-trade had been a tenet of the whig faith; now the attack on slavery itself had the support of both sides of politics - when the meeting was held the resolutions were moved by J.J. Gurney and seconded by John Harvey.

Some time in 1823 Harriet Martineau, who that year attained the age of twenty one, sent Simon the manuscript of her first book, *'Devotional Exercises, by a Lady'*. She was still doubtful of her powers and too shy to allow it to appear under her own name. The Martineau and Wilkin families had long been acquainted and Simon was well known to her brother Thomas, who had encouraged her to write the book, as a fellow-member of the Society of United Friars. The *Devotional Exercises,* which sold for half - a - crown, aroused sufficient interest for a second edition to be printed in the next year. Three years later Simon again printed for her a little book, *'Addresses with Prayers and Original Hymns for the use of Families and Schools, by a Lady'*, a book which gave much pleasure to her father who was then in declining health. Soon after this an acquaintance put her in touch with Houlston of Wellington in Shropshire who perhaps offered her better terms than Simon was prepared to do and her numerous writings were thenceforth printed elsewhere.

Another notable Norwich character for whom Simon printed a book at this time was the Rev. George Beaumont, minister of Ebenezer Chapel, Ber Street. Beaumont was an enthusiastic politician whose attacks against those he thought enemies of the working classes had resulted in his ejection from the Methodist New Connection. When there was trouble between the weavers and manufacturers, he was a frequent speaker at the mass-meetings of the former whose ills he attributed chiefly to the activities of London out-riders - harpies, he called them, ranging the country to get bargains from needy tradesmen who must have money, and so driving down the price of cloth. He was a man who liked to have an enemy to oppose and was just now contending for the orthodox faith against a Swedenborgian preacher.

In October 1824 the premises in the Haymarket received a Royal visit. The occasion arose thus. R.M. Bacon, Simon's former partner in the ill-fated paper-mill, was a musical enthusiast and had for some time been urging upon the Governors of the Norfolk and Norwich Hospital the desirability of a Grand Musical Festival as a money-raiser for that institution. At length he won the support of Edward Taylor - a former Sheriff of Norwich, later to become Gresham Professor of Music - who persuaded his kinsman, Philip Meadows Martineau, to propose the matter to the Hospital Board. All manner of snags arose, from

trouble with the City Committee over the gas lighting of
St Andrew's Hall to difficulties in engaging artists.
Catalani, the desired singer, would only come if she were
allowed to bring six other singers and to receive payment
of all her expenses, plus half the proceeds of the Festival,
terms which the committee was entirely unwilling to entertain. Other artists were engaged and the Festival was
successfully staged in September 1824. The King had consented to be named as Patron of the Festival, the Royal
Dukes - York, Sussex and Gloucester - Vice Patrons. The
Duke of Sussex actually came to Norwich and attended all
six concerts. His Royal Highness was an idol of the
Norwich whigs. He had always deviated from the politics
of his family. At the age of six his father, George III,
had him locked in his nursery and sent supperless to bed
for wearing the wrong colours during an election. A long
sojourn in Germany failed to change his views. Apart from
his politics he was something of a scholar with an especial
interest in Biblical subjects. He amassed a library which
included a thousand editions of the Bible and many Hebrew
manuscripts. He had twice visited Norwich before, staying
at the modest house of Alderman Foster in what is now Old
Bank of England Court in Queen Street. This time he was
staying at the Palace with Bishop Bathurst.
    On the Thursday evening of the Festival, the hall
being unduly crowded, he got up from his seat and addressed
the company lamenting that while so many ladies were
standing, so many gentlemen should be enjoying the comfort
of their seats. He hoped they would do him the honour to
follow the example he was about to set them, whereupon he
quitted his chair and sat on the floor of the gallery - an
act of gallantry which was greeted with huzzas from all
over the hall. After the last oratorio on the Friday
morning the Prince visited the Public Library. He had also
promised to visit the Literary Institution and that same
day their committee met to plan for the occasion. He was
to be received on the morrow at 11 am by the President and
Committee. The doors would be kept closed till his arrival
and the reception party would be admitted through Simon's
premises. Thirty years later Simon recollected the
occasion and wrote:
    "When the Duke of Sussex visited Bishop Bathurst, his
    lordship conducted the Duke to see the Institution,
    where he was met by the President, Colonel Harvey, and
    by most of the literary members of the Society, many of
    whom were presented to his Royal Highness, their respec-
    tive works being placed in his hands. Amongst these
    was the 'Clavis Pentateuchi' of which the Duke took
    especial notice, falling into a long and energetic con-
    versation on the Hebrew points and other kindred matters.
    It was remarked that Mr Kinghorn did not hesitate to
    criticise, though in the most courteous manner, some of
    the Duke's observations. Dr Adam Clarke was mentioned
    by his Royal Highness as a 'profoundly learned man'.
    'Does it not seem to your Royal Highness', was the reply,
    'that Dr Clarke's learning was rather extensive than
    profound?'.... Mr Kinghorn afterwards remarked that the
    Duke's acquaintance with Hebrew seemed to be very

considerable."(3)

The Duke who was a huge figure 6' 4" high must have
had to bow his head to pass through the doorways of the
antique building which housed the Literary Institution.
He however agreed to be its patron and expressed his
intention to become a shareholder. He then got into his
carriage which was blocking the entrance to Simon's
premises and amid the cheers of the populace, drove off
for Holkham.

The Duke had very properly treated both the
Libraries alike, but this did not assuage the ill-feeling
subsisting between them. At the Public Library meeting
a few weeks later it was reported that their unpretentious
reception of the Prince had been contrasted disadvantage-
ously with that of 'other public bodies'. In justification
of their proceedings they stated that his Royal Higness
had laid aside Court etiquette to mingle in the liberal
pursuits of the refined - he appeared to value this above
'the shewy appendages of rank and title - the fulsome
ceremonies of public homage and the noisy plaudits of
admiring crowds'.

They unanimously elected him an honorary member of
their library.

The energy and enthusiasm which had given the
Literary Institution so auspicious a start were not quickly
abated. When the committee met in August 1824 to prepare
the business of the Annual Meeting, Simon told them that
several members had discussed the expediency of adding a
Museum to their enterprise and had expressed their willing-
ness to present specimens. The committee was pleased
with the idea though they had doubts about the financial
implications. At the Annual Meeting in October the secretary read a communication inviting the members to authorise
their committee to adopt such measures as might best
promote the establishment of a Museum and might render it
of the greatest avail and most general utility and yet of
the least possible expense to the funds of the Institution.
The members referred the matter to a committee whose
members were Sir James Edward Smith, G. Sothern, a chemist
and fellow-deacon of Smith at the Octagon, Dr Evans an
Edinburgh M.D. and hero of the Peninsula War who had
settled in Norwich thereafter, William Stark brother of
the artist, Joseph Sparshall a Quaker wine-merchant and
member of Simon's one-time Entomological Society, and
three others already well known to us - Richard Taylor,
Thomas Brightwell and William Youngman, with Simon as
secretary.

Early in December 1824 a special General Meeting
was called to hear the committee's report that the establishment of a collection of subjects in Natural History,
Mineralogy, Geology, Coins and ancient or curious Works
of Art would be highly advantageous in affording much
amusement and scientific instruction to the inhabitants
of the County and City. Sir James Edward Smith proposed
that a Museum be established under the auspices of the
Norfolk and Norwich Literary Institution. This was agreed
to subject to a separate admission fee of 5/- per annum,
or £1-10-0. for a family to the proposed collection. A

prospectus was printed pointing out that Norwich from its central situation as capital of East Anglia and from the advantages it enjoyed in institutions for the promotion of useful knowledge, offered itself unquestionably as focus for a local museum. Botany, Zoology, Entomology, Ornithology, Geology, Mineralogy, Conchology, in short all branches of Natural History, exotic as well as British were proposed as subjects. It would also be a depositary for local antiquities, coins and curious or rare works of art.

The committee appointed to launch the new venture included Sparshall and Sothern, John Taylor another deacon of the Octagon and composer of the song 'The Trumpet of Liberty' celebrating the French Revolution, John Chambers who was engaged in compiling his compendious 'General History of Norfolk', the Rev. Joseph Carter of St John's College, Oxford and Simon Wilkin with Richard Taylor as secretary and William Youngman as treasurer.

The Museum Committee hired a room in the Haymarket from Simon at £13 a year plus £2 for coals. In January 1825 they bought a collection of eighty birds for £12; in February a Spoonbill for 50/-. The cases for the display of the specimens were now ready and William Youngman wrote round to likely donors saying that they were now prepared to receive such items as their friends might be disposed to present. Most members of the committee obliged - Richard Taylor and Thomas Brightwell both sent shells; George Sothern minerals from Cornwall and Derbyshire; John Chambers various minerals and a hybrid pheasant; Joseph Sparshall insects and a hummingbird's nest; William Stark ammonites cut and polished. Simon gave a Limoges dish which was illustrated as frontispiece to the Museum's first catalogue; the Rev. Joseph Carter a gorget and helmet of feathers and teeth from the South Sea Islands - an item which long retained its interest for it was loaned in 1948 to the Canterbury Museum in New Zealand and twelve years later sold with other early acquisitions to the Liverpool City Museum to make good collections lost in the blitz. Other gifts from friends in Norwich, Yarmouth and the county and from London included the skin and skull of a polar bear, skulls and skeletons of other animals, bird's eggs, reptiles and fish, coins and curios from Egypt, India and China. John Chambers tells us that some members contributed whole days to the arrangement of the collection while others presented every article from their rooms worthy of preservation. By May (1825) all was ready and on Monday May 9th the doors were opened to the subscribers from 11 am to 4 pm.

That May (1825) Simon asked the Institution to change its Reading Room for a larger room in the house next door, an arrangement which was agreed to. The room had two fireplaces over one of which was hung an engraved portrait of the President, John Harvey, and a map of Norfolk and Suffolk; over the other a geological map of England and Wales. Parts of the walls were shelved, the rest coloured with a neutral tinted watercolour.

The reason for Simon requiring the Reading Room was no doubt an impending change in his domestic circumstances

54

- he was about to get married. Ten years earlier he had
travelled the country in search of a wife. Now, on July
18th 1825, he was married at Costessey Church to Emma
daughter of John Culley who had taken over the mill there,
after his bankruptcy. The Culleys were a noted dissenting
family, descended from Richard Culley who in 1717 had been
the founding pastor of the Meeting Hill Baptist Church at
Worstead. Before moving to Costessey John Culley had
farmed land at Ringland. He paid tithe to parson Woodforde
and for many years was a regular attendant at the good parson's Tithe Audit Feast, where the company sat down at half
past three and had seldom dispersed by midnight. He took
a minor part in county politics, more than once signing
requisitions to the High Sheriff to convene meetings to
consider the distressed state of agriculture and chairing
meetings in support of Thomas William Coke and his associates. At the time when he signed the marriage register
he was engaged in the business for which he is best remembered - the provision of a new Corn Hall in Norwich. He
had suggested the erection of such a hall a year earlier
and had chaired a number of meetings of millers and other
interested parties in furtherance of the idea. Unfortunat-
ely he fell foul of a formidable adversary in the person of
Alderman Crisp Brown, himself a Corn Merchant, who wanted
the Corporation to take over the scheme. John Culley in
the end had the support of the majority of interested parties and his plan prevailed. The Corn Exchange was ultimately built by Philip Barnes for a consortium of merchants
in a new development which he, Barnes, was promoting which
was given the name Exchange Street. The building was
opened in 1828 when the Corn Growers and Buyers arranged
for John Culley to sit for his portrait to John Jackson R.A.
as a testimony to his effort in providing the building.
According to the Norwich Mercury Jackson's painting of
Mr Culley's head was excellent but the figure was totally
different from the character, manner and deportment of that
gentleman. We know little of Emma but as John Culley's
marriage to her mother, Lucy Paul, took place in 1793 she
must have been several years younger than her husband. In
the days of his 'campaign' Simon had written to Kinghorn of
his determination not to marry anyone who was not 'renewed
by Grace'. He adhered to his intentions - Emma had been
baptised on profession of her faith in November 1820.
        Simon had planned a wedding tour to the continent
intending to publish an account of it which he hoped would
pay his expenses and, as he said, make him more known.
The happy couple were to be accompanied by Emma's parents
and Thomas Brightwell and his wife - after the loss of
Simon's sister he had married Anne Hawkins who had accompanied his first wedding tour - and Mary Youngman, daughter
of Simon's former partner, as a friend for Emma. The party
was also to include a Mr Watts, who knew the intended
route, and George Lewis*, who was to make drawings for the

*George Robert Lewis (1782-1871) had illustrated Dr Dibdin's
Tour through France and Germany published in 1821. His
illustrations were admired and it was said of the book that
it would have been a capital volume if there had been no
letter-press. *D.N.B.*

proposed publication.

Simon was unwell at the time of his wedding. He wrote:

"I was told that at the altar my lips were as pale as my face."

Despite this the party set out next day, travelling in an ex-stage coach in which they were to make the tour. The weather was very hot and Simon acting on advice took some opium.

"This however by mistake of the apothecary was a double dose; and though it charmed away all feeling of pain - yet brought a perspiration and vomiting of some hours continuance which made me a dreadful subject for travelling. Travel however I did and we reached Hockerill at about ten o'clock. Had I travelled five miles longer I should have fainted or to judge by my feelings - I might have died. They all say they never saw such a spectre! Sad work this for a bridegroom to wear such an aspect."

At Hockerill they stayed with a kinsman who summoned his medical attendant to the invalid. The doctor prescribed calomel and the black draught and sent the patient on with a supply of pills. Having regard for the heat they went slowly to avoid wearing out the horses. After another stop at Epping they reached the Ship Inn, Tower Stairs, on Friday night July 22nd in time for bed. The Steam Packet, the Earl of Liverpool, was due to leave for Ostend at 4 am - in the event the party was not embarked till 7 am. The unsocial hour made for bad tempers and there was a quarrel between Brightwell and Watts. Lewis failed to join the party at all, but the rest with their luggage and the carriage were got on board. Simon wrote:

"Down the Thames all was smooth and pleasant, the various objects though known acquired additional interest because we were leaving them. Greenwich Hospital was the principal and I placed it in my memory in order to refer to it in my travels as a comparison with buildings of the same character abroad. Passed several Gibbets with the Dreadful spectacle of pirates who after being executed at Execution Dock were carried out to a dismal swampy place on the banks of the Thames."

When the vessel got out into the ocean nearly all the passengers suffered from sea-sickness though Simon was happily immune. He lay on deck all night beside his wife, doing what he could to help her and her mother and sometimes laughing hysterically at the antics of other afflicted passengers. At 5 am on the Sunday morning the Steam Packet docked at Ostend. Brightwell noted that the stink of the place was inconceivable - snuff had become a necessity of life. Simon, feeling better, sat down and wrote to Kinghorn a long description of the journey. He sent his love to the 'young men' - Josiah Fletcher and his associates - with instructions that he did not wish to hear a word about business of an uncomfortable kind unless it were necessary. He looked optimistically to the future:

"I am surrounded with kind friends and may look forward with the blessing of God to the enjoyment of my tour. The prospect however of this is absolutely trifling in comparison with that which I look forward to in the quiet

56

repose of home with dear Emma. It seems to me that I shall feel that I never yet have had any idea of what happiness means."

Four 'cartish-looking horses' were roped to the carriage and the party rattled along the pavé to Bruges. There they shipped the carriage with some difficulty on a barge and proceeded by water to Ghent. They went on via Antwerp (where they admired the works of Rubens) to Brussels. Enquiring at a bookshop about a visit to Waterloo they were told by the bookseller that it was a subject too full of horror to be thought of - carts full of wounded had been brought in and streams of blood ran in the streets. When they did visit the battlefield they were met by children offering skulls, buttons and other relics for sale; but the Château de Hougement reminded them of Bowthorpe Hall. At Liége they had the first beefsteaks since leaving England. At Cologne on a Sunday they heard a full orchestra of performers at Mass in the unfinished Cathedral but did not appreciate the worship - 'a complete specimen of Catholic mummery' noted Thomas Brightwell. They travelled up the Rhine, admiring the castles, vineyards and old towns -
'little old gothic cities as old as Noah, as fresh in their antiquity and undefiled by modern embellishments as an antiquarian's heart could wish'.

By the bank of the Nah they found stones which were conglomerates of fossil shells and brought back specimens for the new museum. On a Sunday at Wiesbaden they heard an impressive sermon at the French Reformed Church but were offended by the irreverence of the congregation. Returning via Saarbruck and Verdun they spent some days in Paris, obtaining entry to the Louvre and dining on boiled capons in the Boulevard des Italiens. On Sunday September 4th they attended the Rev. Mark Wilks' chapel. Wilks was nephew and namesake of the Norwich preacher and politician. Here they met with a congregation of 150, principally their compatriots, and enjoyed a 'plain, familiar, English address, evangelical and practical'. A week later they were at Amiens. Thence they moved on to Boulogne where Thomas Brightwell bought a collection of upwards of thirty of Rembrandt's smaller etchings from a print shop.* They embarked on a steam boat and landed at Dover on Tuesday September 14th. Simon's intended account of the tour was never published though three years later he printed his brother-in-law's *'Journal of a Tour made by a party of Friends'* from which the above particulars are taken.

From Dover Simon wrote a disconcolate letter to Kinghorn:
"I contemplated in this tour all that could be thought reasonable for me to expect of happiness and enjoyment and perhaps much more. I looked back on the first part of my life which glittered with youthful happiness,

*Brightwell's daughter, Cecilia Lucy, who learned to etch from John Sell Cotman, made copies of these etchings, one of which was accepted as an original Rembrandt by the British Museum until E.T. Daniel corrected the error.
S.D. Kitson, *Life of J.S. Cotman*, p.301

spirits and hope - on its opening when I left you with
the fairest prospects of realising my hopes - on the
clouds of sorrow and adversity which extinguished them
and finally on the seven years of labour and exertion
to which the same character of never failing hope had
impelled me to repair somewhat my situation in life ....
I expected of our Marriage Tour all that circumstances
could command of enjoyment. I was to be surrounded by
most of those I most valued - George Lewis who is perhaps better qualified than any living artist for the
purpose was to accompany us and draw everything most
remarkable ....

My illness, which has never left me, tho' I have
alternated from worse to better - a quarrel between
Mr Brightwell and Mr Watts in London before we started -
the dangerous illness of the latter who was thereby
separated from us - the failure of his negotiation with
Lewis in consequence of my absence from illness, and
finally numberless little sorrows which have befallen
us on the road, have shattered my plan entirely - dis-
appointing us of Switzerland and making the labour to
me far outweigh the pleasure - nay so far that I cannot
look back to any two months of my life in which I have
suffered more unhappiness - and I look forward to the
future endeavouring to have this feeling 'He who knows
what is best for me will do as He seeth best for me'.
A few days will bring us home - where I shall come for
the first time in my life with reluctance and a heavy
heart. I must end or Emma will come and though she
knows that I am unhappy it would make her more unhappy
than she is to read this - therefore I shall practice
my first concealment by sending this off without her
seeing it."(4)

REFERENCES

1. Norwich Mercury, 21 December 1822
2. M.H. Wilkin, op. cit. pp.394 and 395
3. M.H. Wilkin, op. cit. p.454
4. C.B.J. Notes 43. S.W. to J.K. 14 September 1825

Simon married

Despite the gloomy forebodings he suffered on return from his honeymoon, Simon and Emma seem to have settled down happily enough over the shop in the Haymarket. Long afterwards one of Josiah Fletcher's daughters, whose memories went back to the year 1842, wrote down her recollections of the house, describing scenes which had not much changed from the time of Simon's occupancy. She remembered particularly the large drawing-room with its three tall windows looking out on the Haymarket.
"There seems in my memory to have been always something interesting going on below those windows - an election crowd chairing the unfortunate member - processions of boys carrying large loaves as advocates of Free Trade - the yearly progress through the city of the great Dragon, at other times kept in safe custody at the Guildhall - Punch and Judy - and conjurers [who] also played wonderful tricks with balls and hoops."(1)
Simon himself wrote an account of "the great Dragon" as a note to the picture of St George in Sir Thomas Browne's *Vulgar Errors*:
"There has been from time immemorial on Mayor's day at Norwich an annual pageant, the sole remnant of St George's Guild, in which an immense dragon, horrible to view, with hydrahead and wings and scales bedecked in gold and green, is carried about by a luckless wight whose task it is the live-long day by string and pulley from within to open and shut the monster's jaws by way of levying contributions on the gaping multitude especially of youthful gazers with whom it is a matter of half terror, half joy to pop a halfpenny into the opened mouth of Snap (so he is called) whose bow of thanks with long and forked tail high waved in air acknowledges the gift".(2)
Simon continued to take a small part in public affairs, joining a large number of fellow dissenters in November (1825) to requisition the Mayor to call yet another meeting against slavery. This resulted in the formation of 'The Norwich Society for Promoting the immediate Mitigation and final Abolition of Slavery' with a tory, John Harvey, Simon's colleague in the Literary Institution, as President.(3)
The Museum, occupying part of his premises, continued to be a major interest. When the Annual Meeting of

subscribers was held at the Guildhall that November (1825)
Simon took an active part in the discussions, proposing one
of the resolutions and seconding another. Sir James Edward
Smith was elected President. Smith himself maintained a
considerable private museum in his house at 29 Surrey St -
one of the great terrace houses designed and built by the
celebrated Norwich architect, Thomas Ivory - comprising
the Linnean Collection which he had purchased from the
widow of its founder in 1783 and his own additions to it.
Smith's museum was described by Professor Schultz of Land-
shut in Bohemia who visited it in 1824. He saw, he said,
"The Linnaean herbarium in the same order and even
occupying the very cases which had contained it at Upsal
(little as the old-fashioned form of these cabinets
corresponds with the elegant arrangement of Smith's museum); the collection of insects, shells and minerals;....
all these are arranged and preserved by Sir James with a
scrupulous care which borders on a kind of religious
veneration.... Besides the Linnaean herbarium, Sir James
Edward Smith has a large collection of plants of his own
formation, which is especially rich in the productions of
New Holland and Nepaul...."
    Schultz was equally impressed with Smith himself;
"I have rarely beheld a more noble countenance; one
indicative of such candour, simplicity and kindness,
united with so much clearness of intellect...."(4)
    At the Annual Meeting the newly-elected President
spoke about the benefits of such an institution. It was
not merely to be considered as an object of amusement but
as a means of collecting a mass of authority by which
doubtful points would be set at rest and proper appelations
established, thus rendering it a useful study for the young
who would by this means acquire a taste for solid information and have their attention turned, not to the study
of the useful arts alone, but to the great First Cause of
all.(5)
    Following the Annual Meeting the Rev. Thomas Drum-
mond wrote to the paper to advocate the admission of
strangers to the Museum with an entrance fee of 1/-. The
collection, he thought, surpassed anything nearer than
London except for the deposits at the University of Cambridge and if his suggestion were adopted few people would
visit Norwich without seeing it.(6) Drummond's plan was not
adopted though the committee did open the Museum to the
public on a number of special occasions such as Sessions
Week and Tombland Fair. A little later on (May 1827) they
extended admission to schools paying a subscription of
£1.10.0 a year. This entitled Masters and Mistresses to
bring parties of twenty scholars at a time.
    In its early days any attendance the Museum required
was presumably provided from Simon's staff but in December
1825 the Committee felt justified in appointing a full-time
'curator and arranger'. Simon offered to spare Henry Denny
who was in his employ as a draftsman. Henry was a keen
entomologist. Simon had just published his *Monographia Psel-
ophidarum et Scydmaenidarum Britanniae*, illustrated by plates
depicting the beetles described, beautifully drawn and engraved by Denny himself. The museum had already purchased

his collection of insects for £10. When the committee met
on January 5th 1826 Simon had changed his mind and told
them that Denny could not be spared. But he did not long
retain Henry Denny's services for he was shortly appointed
Sub-Curator to the Museum of the Literary and Philosophical Society of Leeds, at a salary of £80 a year.(7)
Having failed to secure the services of Henry Denny
the committee a week later appointed George Denny, perhaps
his younger brother, at a salary of ten shillings a week.
Exhibits were flowing in from many quarters. John Sell
Cotman gave tiles with heraldic devices which he had
brought back from the palace of William Duke of Normandy
at Caen; Seth Stevenson, various relics including a club,
battle-axe and spear from New Zealand and a garnet from
the rocks near Mount Simplon; Richard Taylor, a large
fossil found near Cromer; J.J. Gurney, a male bittern;
Mr Blofeld of Hoveton, various birds' eggs; Mr Wombwell
of the famous menagerie, a young lion; and Simon himself,
specimens of metallic 'oxyds' from his sterotype factory,
to mention only a few. Space was becoming a problem. In
May (1826) Simon offered the Museum a larger room for £40
a year which was agreed to, but by September pressure was
such that another room on the West side of the courtyard,
measuring 38 foot by 20, had to be brought into use. The
rent was increased to £50 a year and the curator's salary
to 12/- a week. His position was no sinecure. He was
directed not to absent himself for dinner between one
o'clock and two, though some months later the committee
agreed that he might do so between three and four o'clock.
In 1828 his salary was increased to 15/- and later his
wife was employed to help keep the place clean at 19/6 a
quarter. George Denny was to remain Curator till 1847.
He seems to have been a modest and self-effacing character
but he was not without abilities. In 1837 the committee
voted him £5 as a slight remuneration for two beautiful
manuscript volumes of Ornithology illustrated by coloured
plates, the production of his own hand. Though not original, these volumes with their seventy coloured drawings
are really works of art and the appellation 'beautiful' is
a just one. They remain at the Museum to this day. Simon
himself continued an enthusiastic collector whether on his
own behalf or for the Museum. In November (1826) he was
in correspondence with W.J. Hooker about acquiring a good
Herbarium. He had an offer of 3,000 specimens for £23.
If they were good, Hooker wrote, this would be dirt cheap -
if bad they might not be worth as many pence. He might
after all get English specimens for the gathering - Swiss
and German plants could be bought cheaply and Mr Bowie, an
able and zealous botanist, was about to go to the interior
of Southern Africa - Simon could write to him using Hooker's
name if he wished.(8) James Bowie to whom Hooker referred
had been to the Cape as Botanical Collector to the Royal
Gardens at Kew. He was recalled in 1823, a vote of the
House of Commons having reduced the sum available for this
service. In 1827 he returned on his own account and, says
the Dictionary of National Biography, 'by many years of
patient labour in the interior of South Africa he enriched
the gardens of Europe'.

Insects continued to be Simon's special interest. He had evidently amassed a considerable collection since his former one had been sold in 1816 for the Museum purchased his insects in 1827 for the substantial sum of one hundred guineas. The Museum was short of cash. Receipts during the year had been no more than £317 and the Committee had made a number of purchases including a 'splendid fossil turtle' for which they had sucessfully competed with Cambridge, York and Manchester. They paid Simon £5 down and agreed to 5% interest on the balance till it could be paid off. This purchase enabled the Norwich Mercury to write that their Cabinet of Insects was superior to any provincial collection in the Kingdom.(9) At this time one of the volunteer enthusiasts helping with the Museum was William Kirby who wrote of it in October 1827,
"The Museum keeps increasing, particularly in Conchology and Fossils. They have recently got a very fine fossil specimen of a Testudo, found at Harwich.... I have been very busily engaged in arranging Mr Brightwell's Coleoptera for the Museum. I am to have duplicates for my trouble."(10)

In 1826 Simon published George Borrow's first book, *Romantic Ballards translated from the Danish*. This year too the local interest in making Norwich a Port brought forth a number of publications. Simon printed *Important Considerations on the Subject of Norwich a Port* by H.B. Disney, the Trinity Pilot at Lowestoft, commending the scheme which, he said, would create an 'asylum harbour' at Lowestoft whereas now there was no secure inlet for the storm-driven mariner between Harwich and the Humber. He also printed *An Abstract of Evidence taken before a Committee of the House of Commons on a Bill for making the river navigable between Lowestoft and Norwich*. The Bill was duly passed in May 1827 and when its protagonists, who had gone to London to witness the event, returned home they were received with great enthusiasm. A crowd came out of the city to meet the Times Coach which was bringing them. Above 150 horsemen were followed by the Mayor and Sheriffs in their carriages. Alderman Crisp Brown the leading supporter of the scheme sat on the box and among those in the coach were Simon's father-in-law John Culley and his brother-in-law Thomas Brightwell. The populace took the horses out of the coach and drew it by hand into the city where houses were decorated with laurels. A bonfire was lighted in the marketplace which the Watch tried and failed to extinguish at midnight. The Mercury spoke of the passing of the Bill as 'the most important event Norwich ever saw', a judgement scarcely borne out by the use made of the navigation when the work was completed.

Meanwhile Simon had been developing his business, adding two new activities - the casting of Stereotype Plates and the manufacture of Printer's Ink. In May 1826 he printed a pamphlet addressed to the Printers and Publishers of Great Britain in which he claimed that the plates cast in his factory were entirely free from defects hitherto judged insuperable, resulting in a brilliant sharpness in the surface of the smallest letter. On January 13th 1827 the Norwich Mercury was printed with his ink. The result was satisfactory but whether the Mercury continued to use it had not been recorded. In May (1827) Simon took Emma on a trip, combining business with pleasure. They went first to Cambridge where a friend escorted her to 'see the lions' while Simon made his business calls. Mr Hodgson was well satisfied with the ink he had had and ordered more; the University Press thought it too stiff and were to be supplied with further samples.

They went on to London, leaving Cambridge at two and arriving at seven at the Bull. Here they refreshed themselves with tea and then set out to seek accommodation for the night. It was 9.30 pm by the time they settled on 'an attick in Cochran's house'. Next day they went on to stay with friends in Camberwell where they were joined by Emma's parents. On Sunday the party went to hear Dr Thomas Chalmers at Edward Irving's fashionable chapel in Regent Square. Chalmers, who then held the Chair of Moral Philosophy at St Andrew's University, had made a great impression when he preached in London ten years earlier, causing Wilberforce to note in his diary that all the world was wild about him, vast crowds were attending his services and even Canning was moved to tears by his oratory. On this occasion, though Simon was unwell and fell asleep in the middle of the discourse, he expressed delight in what he heard and was able to give Kinghorn an account of the drift of the sermon.

From London they went to Windsor where the King was adding a mass of new buildings to the castle - "making Windsor truly a Royal Residence". Simon thought the Chapel "extremely beautiful, the organ and choir delightful". At Oxford Simon failed to sell his ink, but he had other business. His pupil Josiah Fletcher was about to complete his apprenticeship and there was a scheme for him to join printers at Oxford. There was some doubt about his acceptability, being a dissenter, but, Simon charged Kinghorn to tell him,

"He is to be put into the ranks first, as the most likely way to get on - and by making himself useful and necessary by degrees to prepare himself for any circumstance which may remove Mr Collingwood."

They returned to London and then went to Brighton where they found the air of the purest and most delightful kind and their life very even. "The town is spreading", Simon wrote, "on all sides and many extremely fine buildings adding to it - rents are enormous - vivre very extravagant". All the Brighton printers approved his ink and two actually ordered it.(11)

The arrangements for Josiah Fletcher to go to Oxford fell through. Joseph Kinghorn apparently intervened on his behalf and persuaded Simon to find employment for him. Josiah was in London in October when he wrote to thank Kinghorn and to say that he had long wished to stay in Norwich and "accepts the very liberal and handsome proposal of Mr Wilkin with gladness". He was at length taken into partnership and in 1830 books were being published by Wilkin and Fletcher.

Simon was still busy over his ink business. In

October (1827) when Kinghorn was staying with Mr Foster,
the Cambridge Banker, he wrote to ask, would Mr Foster
call with Kinghorn on his customer Mr Hodgson and enquire
whether the ink had arrived safely and gave satisfaction?
The call would inform Mr Hodgson that he, Simon, was known
to such a respectable person as Foster!(12) He wrote too
to W.J. Hooker asking him to find an agent for him in
Glasgow. Hooker was not successful - he approached
Mr Lumsden a wealthy stationer and magistrate but found
him already engaged to a Birmingham supplier.(13) The
ink business grew and needed more space. Simon asked the
Museum to vacate the cellar where their coals were stored
- eventually a compromise was reached and half the cellar
was made over to the ink trade.

That November (1827) Simon made yet another business
trip, leaving home, he said, in a state of mental depression and feverishness. "Travelling commercially abounds
with temptations". He spent the first Sabbath in Leicester
hearing superior sermons from James Parsons of York and
enjoying the society of very pleasant kind people. He
wrote again from Macclesfield on November 21st that he had
spent the next Sabbath in the delightful company of Mr and
Mrs Swinburne; delightful because the lady gossiped of
Kinghorn's youthful days when she had been his playfellow.
He went on to Manchester where, staying at Blackfriars'
Inn, he remembered words Kinghorn used rather frequently
to repeat to him -
"Simon boast not thyself of tomorrow, for thou knowest
not what a day may bring forth".
That night he was obliged to send for a doctor but a great
dose of Castor Oil effected a cure.(14) Simon's health
inclined to be delicate. He often had to consult doctors
at home and when on journeys. One time in London he went
to Sir Astley Cooper, the Norfolk surgeon who had settled
in town where he enjoyed an enormous popularity and was
said to command an income of £15,000 a year. He sent
Simon home with a note to Dr Dalrymple. The patient wrote
to Kinghorn:
"I applied to Astley Cooper who considers it very important to reduce the disease at once or it may terminate
in -- Cancer! -- he thinks it a curious case and as yet
unimportant. But Dalrymple by his direction has been
with me today. Astley Cooper desired me to lie on my
Sofa -- for a month -- to apply leaches twice a week to
take opening medecines and live low -- Dalrymple inter-
prets his directions most rigidly so that I am not to
stir.
I hope you will come over to see me when convenient.
I am puzzling my brain for an employment for this lying
in month."(15)
In March 1828 Simon's old friend Sir James Edward
Smith died at his house in Surrey Street, Norwich. He was
succeeded by Lord Stanley as President of the Linnaean
Society. The Society proposed to raise £4,000 to purchase
Smith's Botanical Collections but the subscriptions fell
far short of the amount required. This caused Simon to
write rather a tart letter to the Secretary promising to
give his £1 provided the whole sum could be raised and

suggesting that the noble President and other leading
subscribers should reopen the subscription list by quin-
tupling their gifts.(16)   In the end the collection was
bought by the Society for £3,000.

Hudson Gurney was approached to succeed Smith as
President of the Norfolk and Norwich Museum.   He refused
the office but shortly afterwards made the Museum a gift
of £50 which the committee made over to Simon in part payment of their debt for the insect collection.   Eventually
Dawson Turner was elected President.

Since 1824 Simon had printed several books and
pamphlets for the Norwich authoress Amelia Opie.   In the
Spring of 1828 he had in hand for her *Detraction Displayed* -
a book on the various modes of detraction, lessening the
merits of others by finding fault, ridicule, mimicry etc.
The book was not a manual of one-up-manship but a warning
against an evil habit.   Amelia had by now joined the
Society of Friends and wanted her book to be in the shops
by May 25th so as to be available to Friends attending
the Yearly Meeting.   J.J. Gurney who exercised much influence over her feared she would have to resort to London
printers to get the job done in time but she wrote to Simon
on March 19th saying she disliked anyone else printing it.
Simon completed the 400 octavo pages of the book in time
and, having regard to her particularity as to the date,
marked the final page 'Printed by S. Wilkin May 16 1828'.

While Simon was hastening *Detraction Displayed* through
the press, he also had in hand the substantial first volume
of William Taylor's *Historic Survey of German Poetry*, com-
pleting the 506 pages of this work on May 15th (1828).
Volumes II and III, each of similar size to the first, were
printed in April 1829 and September 1830 respectively.
Taylor's magnum opus was not wholly successful.   Thomas
Carlyle unkindly suggested that its authentic title might
be 'General Jail-delivery of all Publications and Manuscripts, original or translated, composed or borrowed, on
the subject of German Poetry, by &c.'   Taylor also offended
Sir Walter Scott by making a gratuitous and unfounded
assumption about his name and appending a note to the
translation of one of Goethe's works by William Scott of
Edinburgh - 'no doubt the same person who under the poet-
ical but assumed name of Walter has since become the most
extensively popular of the British writers'.   On receiving
a letter of remonstrance from Sir Walter he promised to
correct his error in any second edition and, if desired,
to publish Scott's letter and his reply in the East Anglian
newspaper 'which is printed by my publishers' - the enterprise with which our next chapter will be concerned.(17)

In Assize Week in August 1828 the Norwich artists
held their annual exhibition for the first time in the
gallery they had erected in the new development of Exchange
Street - 'risking a considerable outlay' as the Mercury
commented, 'for the gratification of the public'.   Simon
went to their exhibition and bought a picture.   He seems
to have had a particular penchant for the works of John
Sell Cotman.   We have seen that in the days of his first
affluence he had acquired a number of Cotman's watercolours which were sold in 1816 to pay his creditors.   Now

in 1828 Cotman, who was teaching at his house in St Martin at Palace Plain, advertised lessons in drawing from 'the best Models of the Antique and Middle Ages, collected during many years with great care and expense....'(18) Using, no doubt, items from this collection John Sell Cotman himself painted a large water-colour, 'The Investigation', a self portrait of the artist with two of his sons dressed in sixteenth century costume and grouped around a table in a room littered with coats of armour, shields and pikes. This picture, which Cotman is said to have rated one of his best drawings, was purchased by Simon to adorn the house in the Haymarket.(19)

An important event took place that October (1828). Simon wrote to Kinghorn -

"I must let you know that dear Emma has brought me a girl - all doing as well as possible. My wife has been in the most perfect health up to the very day - she took her short walk with her brother yesterday in the field and was only unwell in the evening - knocked me up at midnight - Josiah went for the nurse and I finished my night in the next room".

The child was named Emma Mary. A second daughter, Mary Jacomb, was to be born in April 1830 and a son, Martin Hood, in April 1832.

REFERENCES

1. Fletcher family papers, Recollections of Lucy Massey
2. *Sir Thomas Browne's Works*, 1852 edition, Vol. II, p.55
3. Norwich Mercury, 26 November 1825
4. *Transactions of Norfolk and Norwich Naturalists Society*, Vol. IX, p.662
5. Norfolk and Norwich Museum, Minute Book
6. Norwich Mercury, 3 December 1825
7. E. Kitson Clarke, *History of Leeds Philosophical and Literary Society*, p.38
8. Wilkin Papers, 97. W.J.H. to S.W. 26 November 1826
9. Norwich Mercury, 9 August 1828
10. J. Freeman, *Life of Wm Kirby*, p.428
11. Wilkin Papers, 106 and 107. S.W. to J.K. 14 and 29 May 1827
12. C.B.J. Notes 45. S.W. to J.K. 22 October 1827
13. Wilkin Papers, 126. W.J.H. to S.W. 29 December 1828
14. Wilkin Papers, 117. S.W. to J.K. 21 November 1827
15. Wilkin Papers, 134. S.W. to J.K. undated
16. Linnean Society, S.W. to J.E.Bicheno. 6 December 1828
17. J.W. Robberds, *William Taylor of Norwich*, pp.538 and 547
18. Norwich Mercury, 19 January 1828
19. S.D. Kitson, *Life of J.S. Cotman*, p.277

Newspaper proprietor

While Simon's young family was growing up in the heart of Norwich, both city and the country around were seething with discontent. The chaplain of the County Jail could only impute the increase in the number of prisoners there to the incompetency of the labourer's income to purchase sufficient food for himself and his children at current prices.(1) In August (1829) the journeymen weavers memorialised the Mayor - T.O. Springfield - complaining that being only partially employed they could not purchase for themselves and their families but half enough of the common necessaries of life. But the year produced incidents to remind them that their case might be even worse. One Saturday in April a great crowd, many females among them, gathered to witness the hanging of a sheep-stealer and a horse-thief in the Castle Ditches only a stone's throw from the house in the Haymarket. Then in August, John Stratford, a whitesmith, was executed there for poisoning. His case made a great impression and was reported at unusual length in the local papers. J.J. Gurney spent an hour with him on the Sabbath morning before his execution. Stratford told him his fall was due to the abandonment of the Christian faith occasioned by reading Tom Paine and Richard Carlile. Having lost his standard of right and wrong, he had entered into an adulterous relationship with a married woman and then sought to poison her husband. He was repentant and made an edifying exit with a prayer on his lips. J.J. Gurney wrote a tract on Stratford's story and took it to Simon for printing. Ten thousand copies were distributed gratis, presumably at the author's expense, and some more were sold at a penny each. The Mayor advised the weavers to be peaceable though firm - "Respect the laws and their utmost power shall be exerted to support you". The support of the law unhappily brought no alleviation of hunger. In November (1829) some unemployed weavers paraded the streets preceded by fife and drum and a shuttle draped with black, but not many had spirit enough to support the demonstration. Some masters were now offering work at lower prices than those long agreed and confirmed in 1822. The more militant weavers were determined to maintain the agreed rates and the fat was in the fire when the Court of Guardians stated they would not pay relief to weavers refusing work offered at a reduced price. The weavers held a protest

meeting on Mousehold Heath at which indignation was expressed particularly against the two leading Guardians,
Thomas Athow a stonemason and William Geary a cheesemonger. "It is an abominable fudge", said a speaker,"for
a stonemason and a cheesemonger to settle the prices for
weaving". The crowd then descended on the city and broke
the windows of Athow's and Geary's houses. In January
(1830) when the Guardians sought to erect looms in the
workhouse to employ weavers on their own terms, a crowd of
3,000 assembled on the road, seized the looms and threw
them into the river. Conferences took place between the
Weaver's Committee and the Manufacturers and when these
produced no positive results some extremists took to acts
of violence. Masked men broke into William Springall's
house in St Augustine's, cut the work from seven looms in
his attics and when he tried to intervene fired a pistol
and wounded him. Mr Wright, another manufacturer, was
attacked in the street with vitriol and lost the sight of
an eye. Later on when Richard Nockolds was awaiting
execution for stack-burning he confessed to being the
ringleader in the attacks on Springall and Wright. He had
begun his career of crime during the disputes between the
weavers and masters. Through reading Cobbett and Carlile
he had come to entertain a bitter hatred of every order
of society above his own.(2)

By February (1830) the weavers were reported to be
accepting work at reduced prices. William Geary, the
Guardian and cheesemonger, put his views down in writing
and took them to Simon to be printed under the heading
*'An earnest Appeal to the Weavers of Norwich on the passing Events
of the present awful Crisis'*. He attributed the troubles to
a change of fashion banishing bombazines and crapes from
the market. He welcomed the growing silk trade as a means
of alleviation. Combinations to keep up wages he thought
unsound in principle, mischievous in practice and incapable
of attaining their object, leading to outrage and violence.
Geary was answered by a weaver, J.W. Greeves, in a pamphlet
printed by John Jarrold's rival press. He defended the
weavers' right to hold out for a price; attributed the
evils of the situation to ruinous competition -- "the
tiger-like ferocity which caused one master to prey on the
vitals of another" -- and condemned the silk trade as no
more nor less than the introduction of work at lower levels
of pay. The only remedy against pauperism, he thought, was
cooperation.

In May (1830) with the death of George IV impending,
the weavers hoped a market for black goods would develop
and planned, if trade were brisk enough, to enforce a
demand for higher wages by a strike. In the event the late
king's popularity proved not sufficient to justify their
plan.

With the death of George IV parliament was dissolved
and a general election called. The blue-and-white candidates for Norwich, favouring reform, were R.H. Gurney and
Robert Grant; the orange -and- purple, Jonathon Peel and Sir
Charles Ogle. The election was fought on July 29th and
30th (1830) not only with votes but with stones and staves.
On the marketplace the blue-and-white voting booth was

damaged; that of the orange-and-purples wholly demolished. One unlucky onlooker was hit on the head by a stone and died in hospital. Despite the risks run by the voters there was a record poll and the reformers were well on top. Both Joseph Kinghorn and Simon Wilkin went to record their votes for Robert Grant, refraining from supporting R.H. Gurney no doubt on account of his marital irregularities -- he had run off with the wife of his neighbour Joseph Muskett and had recently had to pay £2,000 damages awarded by the court to the aggrieved husband. Whatever scruples Simon may have had this circumstance does not seem to have affected Gurney's popularity with the majority of the voters -- he polled nearly 100 votes more than did his running-mate.

Simon who had now taken Josiah Fletcher into partnership received yet another document on the situation to print from W.H. Meteyard. His remedies were - the Repeal of the Corn Laws, the Game Laws and the Poor Law; the reduction of the Army and Navy; the abolition of all monopolies, duties, patents and corporations; a national system of education and the extension of the franchise to all males over 21 not having received parochial relief since the last election.

The situation in the country was no better than that in the town. Wilkin and Fletcher printed Thomas Watts's *'Present evil and alarming Prospects of the Agricultural Population with a safe easy and effectual Remedy'*. The remedy proposed was an improved agriculture bringing into use vast areas of land at present unbroken. In Norfolk, Watts says, it is a rule to allow ten acres out of a hundred for farm fencing whereas in his judgement four would be amply sufficient. The labour to cultivate additional lands could be found by abolishing the Poor's Rate so far as the able-bodied are concerned and requiring them to work for the parish.

Against this background of discontent, in October 1830, Simon Wilkin and Josiah Fletcher involved themselves in the enterprise of publishing a weekly newspaper. For two generations past Norwich had been served by two weekly newspapers, the Norwich Mercury now edited by Simon's former partner Richard Mackenzie Bacon and generally taking a whig stand point, and the Norfolk Chronicle, the organ of the tory party, conducted by Seth William Stevenson who had been Sheriff of the city in 1828 and was to be Mayor in 1832. Rex Stedman who studied the Norfolk newspapers in some depth, considered that Bacon made the Mercury one of the leading provincial organs of liberal opinion and was one of the most cultivated editors of his time.(3) Stevenson, apart from his tory politics, was more conservative in his presentation of the news. While Bacon in his enthusiasm for music and the drama would sometimes devote space to these items to the exclusion of other local news Stevenson was more consistent in his content and layout.

Neither of these weekly papers supported the views of the more radical politicians and from time to time attempts had been made to remedy this. Back in 1794 a society of Norwich gentlemen had published the Cabinet, a monthly magazine comprising original pieces on topics connected with the science of civil polity, law and the

constitution, but after a year this was given up as being
dangerous. Then in 1803 an attempt was made to float a
third weekly newspaper, the Iris, in the radical interest.
The editorship was offered to Robert Southey the poet at
a salary of £1.11.6 a week - William Taylor told him the
printer could probably be got to pay £2.2.0. In the end
Taylor undertook the task himself, though Southey wrote,
"I cannot be satisfied that W. Taylor should be a newspaper editor; that he who should be employed in preparing
dishes for the daintiest palates should be making wash
for swine".

Nevertheless Southey later averred in a letter to
Taylor that the Iris was not only a very interesting paper
but the only interesting one. The first number came out on
February 6th 1803. About 1,000 were printed and Taylor
wrote, "many people gave shillings in the afternoon to
those who had bought it for 6d in the morning". Despite
this hopeful start the Iris was not for long able to make
ends meet. It lasted nearly two years and finished with
its hundredth number.

Now, a quarter of a century later, as the agitation
for the reform of Parliament gathered force another attempt
was made under the title of 'The East Anglian, or Norfolk,
Suffolk and Cambridgeshire; Norwich, Lynn and Yarmouth
Herald', with Wilkin and Fletcher as printers. The first
number appeared on Tuesday October 12th 1830, a tabloid
of eight pages 16" by 11". Six months later the East
Anglian reverted to the format of the older papers - 4
pages 24" by 18". The editor chosen for the new paper was
Thomas Starling Norgate who had been a leading contributor
to the Cabinet back in 1794. Norgate is chiefly remembered
as founder (in 1829) of the Norfolk and Norwich Horticul-
tural Society. Many Norwich weavers and other artizans
took an interest in cultivating flowers - perhaps an
inheritance from ancestors who had been immigrants from
the Low Countries. One of Norgate's aims had been to
encourage this habit and prizes for cottagers was an aspect
of the Society's work from the beginning. He now took up
his pen and wrote an initial leading article, adorned with
classical allusions, marking out the field in which it had
to operate, describing its competitors and laying down its
policy - an article which we may summarise as follows:
It is more than a century since the herald Mercury came
among us. The wings which decorate his head may indicate
an occasional flightiness of speculation, an airiness of
fancy and volatility of style. Old Chronos has long been
content to exchange etheral viands for the solid beef and
plum pudding of Norfolk. He enjoys his joke still - as
Homer says the celestials love laughing. After the failure of former attempts to establish a third newspaper in
Norwich it may be deemed presumptuous to repeat the
experiment - but the presumption is in favour of success,
grounded on the increasing interest which an increasing
population takes in public affairs. The East Anglian is
but mortal yet does he aspire to exercise vigilance.
Argus the God of Vigilance had 100 eyes - we hope to sur-
pass him. We shall look sharp for intelligent correspondents and for information on subjects of local and

political interest; marriages, births and deaths, the
state of the markets, of the funds, the crops, the
weather &c, &c, will be duly recorded. We must not
forget to look sharp for subscribers to our paper and
for advertisements, the golden pinions to sustain its
flight.
        Adequate foundations had been laid for the success
of the venture. London agents had been appointed and the
provision of the 'golden pinions' of advertisement can-
vassed. In fact advertisements occupied about a quarter
of the space available. These included two local Insurance
Companies - the General Equitable Fire Office, supported
by Gurney's Bank, and the New Equitable Assurance Society,
supported by Harvey's Bank. The latter cast a jaundiced
eye on the rival Norwich Union - 'In preference to a vague
system in which every Insurer is a partner, no mutual
liability is incurred here'. Simon's old partner, William
Youngman, advertised his Porter, Ales and Spirits; William
Taylor, protagonist of the last-attempted radical weekly,
his *Historic Survey of German Poetry* in three volumes, while
various tradesmen offered the whole gamut of regular re-
quirements from superior sausages to suits of clothes to
be made at six hours notice. Societies advertised their
annual meetings, schools their curriculum and fees, the
Octagon Chapel its evening lectures. Sporting Intelligence
included Horse Racing and sometimes Cock-fighting. In the
local news was a report of the Quarterly meeting of the
Court of Guardians, the monthly Museum Committee when a
profusion of valuable donations were received, and a public
dinner of the Orange and Purple Club. An Agricultural
section pointed out the dangers of a free import of corn -
an old theme of Simon's to which the East Anglian was often
to revert. Later it was conceded that when by reduction
of rents, rates, tithes and taxes the English farmer should
be placed on a level with those of other countries then the
Corn Laws might be abolished.(4)
        The East Anglian took a high view of the importance
of newspapers:
    'The press is the most powerful moral engine in the world
    .... We may assert .... that it is omnipotent at least
    in England, in France and America, the three freest
    countries in the world, and the freest because of the
    omnipotence of the press'.(5)
        Experience was to temper this view. After the long
struggle for the Reform Bill --
    'The press can do nothing or little against public opin-
    ion; supported by it, it can do anything. It does not
    regulate but is regulated by public opinion'.(6)
        The policy of the new paper would, it proclaimed,
be 'Abstraction from Party, Adhesion to Principle'. The
Principle was generally what might be called liberal. Vote
by ballot was frequently advocated, an advanced notion
which even the Mercury regarded as premature. After the
1832 election --
    'We have heard of so many flagrant acts of intimidation
    and down-right bribery in the course of the present con-
    test for this city that all our prepossessions in favour
    of the Ballot are confirmed .... Can it be supposed that

71

a poor weaver having a wife and children without sufficient fire or food or clothing and without employment
to earn them should always resist the temptation of a
bribe?'(7)

While the paper did not advocate the abolition of
the monarchy it took the old radical stance of lauding the
superiority of the American Constitution -- contrasting
the King's Speech at the opening of Parliament, giving
the least possible information in the least intelligible
language, with the President's message to the Congress of
the United States, giving an explicit and ample narrative
of measures past and in agitation. The performance of the
monarch himself was also criticised --
'George IV usually had a slight attack of gout a day or
two before the assembly of Parliament which lasted just
long enough to prevent his attendance .... not so long
as to interfere with the pleasure of a dinner party or
grand ball at the palace at the latter end of the
week.'(8)

Among the agricultural community machine-breaking
and incendiarism were now rife, so much so that the Norwich
Union was refusing to insure farms which possessed the
hated threshing-machines. The East Anglian commented --
'He who has nothing to gain from the propitiousness of
the seasons or the fertility of the soil; who lives from
day to day on the lowest wages and the sad pittance of
the parish purse; who has no means of providing in the
period of manhood against the approaching necessities
of sickness, decrepitude and old age, can hardly be
expected to feel an interest in the preservation of that
established system of social order which excludes him
from all the benefits of society.... The present course
of destruction must be stopped by a resolute and strong
hand, that must be done first and being done no pains
should be spared to open for the working classes some
new channel for their industry capable of maintaining
them in comfort.'(9)

And the following week --
'Privation, when unendurable will work its own cure and
wreak vengence on the state of society to which it owes
its existence. Let those who have drawn prizes in the
lottery of life take heed of this and contemplate the
numerical strength of their less fortunate fellow beings
to whom blanks are allotted.'(10)

The paper had to admit that militancy sometimes
paid --
'A few short months ago the magistrates of every village
were busy swearing in Special Constables to keep the
hungry peasantry from breaking machines and from extort-
ing at the point of the pitchfork higher wages than they
had before. Terms of capitulation were in most places
agreed to to the advantage of the insurgents'.(11)

In the city too there was hunger and discontent.
In November (1830), when a Common Hall was called to
petition Parliament for relief from the duty on sea-borne
coals, the East Anglian wrote of a relief which would go
to the personal comfort of the poor -- 'This is one of
the few subjects on which no diversion of sentiment is to

be anticipated'. A week later, ruefully -- 'We certainly must disclaim all pretensions to prophecy'. When Col. Harvey, not long since the idol of the weavers, rose to propose the resolutions all order was destroyed and confusion reigned. A placard was exhibited by Mr Dover, a member of the weavers' committee, inscribed -- 'Machinery and starvation; cheap coals support the Power-Looms'. Among the clamour cries were heard of -- 'No Corn Laws', 'Reform in Parliament' and Down with machinery'. It proved impossible to restore order and the Mayor dissolved the meeting. John Dover later came into prominence as a leader of the Chartists. His most remarkable achievement was in taking over a meeting for which the tories had hired St Andrew's Hall. He succeeded in packing the hall with his supporters, proposed Matthew Smith, a working weaver, as chairman in place of Col. Harvey the tory nominee, and when Smith had been appointed by acclamation of the meeting secured a resolution calling for universal adult male suffrage. His stormy career came to an end in 1843 when he was sentenced to fourteen years transportation for receiving stolen silk.

Dissidents in city and county sometimes coalesced. In December (1830) a Norwich mob marched to Hellesdon to break Mr Gowing's threshing-machine and then returned to attack Willett's bombazine factory in St Martin's-at-Oak where they cut the work from twenty six looms.(12)

Opposition to the use of machinery was not confined to the machine-breakers who took the law into their own hands. In January 1831 Wilkin and Fletcher printed a pamphlet for G.C. Burrows of Norwich who argued that threshing-machines were the cause of a direct loss to the full extent of the agricultural poor-rate and that factories were a certain high-road to the destruction of health, morality, virtue and domestic industry. "Machinery is a many-headed reptile, born of Ambition, her foster-child is Starvation". He advocated the restraint of machinery by law if not its abolition.

In this time of ferment the East Anglian did not advocate a levelling process -
"There are multitudes who yet believe that all accumulations of property are lawful plunder to the indigent and that all distinctions of rank are derogatory to the natural and primitive equality of man .... The schoolmaster has yet to teach unnumbered multitudes that gradation in Society is essential to its very existence".(13)

At the County Sessions in January 1831 no less than sixty prisoners were charged with machine-breaking and rioting. In the first case the jury found the defendant not guilty but unwisely added the explanation that their decision was reached because there was only one witness. The chairman told them that unless they thought the witness came to perjure himself they should accept his evidence. They retired again but decided to stick to their guns and returned a verdict of not guilty raising applause in the court. Despite public sympathy many of the accused were inevitably found guilty and received sentences varying from six months imprisonment to seven years transportation.

In Norwich the operative weavers began to look to

Parliamentary Reform as a panacea for their ills. At a
meeting in St Andrew's Hall on January 19th 1831 their
chairman, J.W. Greeves, made an eloquent plea for Radical
Reform which alone, he said, could prevent tumult and
disorder.
  "If this cannot be achieved without meddling with the
  established institutions of the country, then you may
  rest assured that these establishments will not long
  endure".
      Lord John Russell introduced the first Reform Bill
into the Commons on March 1st 1831, proposing to disin-
franchise 60 'rotten boroughs' with less than 2,000 inhabitants and to reduce to single member representation
another 47 with less than 4,000. Additional seats were to
be allotted to London and the new manufacturing towns.
The East Anglian published a supplement giving Russell's
speech at length. On the whole the editor thought Ministers had done their duty and given us reason to glory in
a peaceful revolution. The effect, as he correctly fore-
saw, would be to place the elective franchise principally
in the middle classes. The whole country, he said, was on
the side of the Bill except for a hundred or two harpies
powerful by the abuses the country wishes to be rid of.
This estimate of support for Reform was somewhat over-
optimistic. In Norwich itself there was a backlash against
the Bill. Hitherto the body of Freemen of the City with
the Freeholders had elected its two representatives in
Parliament. Any reform would remove their monopoly if it
did not destroy their rights. On the lowest consideration
the freemen were in danger of losing their 'septennial
bribe' for even those who were firm party members and
would not sell their votes to the other side expected a
gratuity or at least free entertainment from their own
party during the period of an election. The East Anglian
interviewed a weaver who stated that he had always voted
blue-and-white except once when he was 'cooped' on Wroxham
Broad and once when the blue-and-whites were so short of
cash that they had no chance of winning, when he thought
it foolish to throw away a vote by which he could earn a
handsome compliment from the other side.(14) 'Cooping',
which meant forcible detention to prevent known supporters
of the opposite side from voting in elections, was a common
practice. Voters were often 'cooped' at Inns in the vil-
lages surrounding Norwich; sometimes on boats on the river
or broads.
      In the local elections of 1830 the tories had
succeeded in wresting from the whigs the majority of the
Common Council. In March 1831 they consolidated their
position and tory speakers believed that a great accession
of strength had come from their known opposition to many
parts of the Reform Bill.(15) The Bill passed its second
reading by one vote in the Commons and was then defeated
in Committee. Some 500 Norwich Bankers, Merchants and
Traders signed a declaration deploring the plan to defeat
the "glorious measure of constitutional reform" and pledg-
ing themselves in the event of a dissolution of Parliament
to re-elect the city's representatives, R.H. Gurney and
Robert Grant, who were supporters of the measure. Simon

Wilkin was a signatory to this declaration as were his
brother-in-law Thomas Brightwell, his father-in-law John
Culley and T.S. Norgate, the editor of the East Anglian.
The King did dissolve Parliament, thereby acquiring popularity with the reformers. Of the election in the Spring
of 1831 the East Anglian wrote --
'Although a General Election necessarily puts the country
into a high state of excitement, we certainly never
remember it in such a state of excitement as to extent
or character as at the present moment .... It is a
struggle of the people of this free country for the
recovery of their lost right -- for the ascendency of
popular representation'.
The paper went on to quote the words of Thomas
William Coke, 'In the fearful crisis we have now reached,
there is no issue except by Reform or Revolution'.(16)
After the election the paper was able gleefully to report
a two to one majority for the 'friends of Reform' - Gurney
and Grant - over the 'supporters of Corruption'. The
Government, its support increased by the election, now
introduced a second version of the Reform Bill. All that
summer the Bill moved haltingly through the Commons until
on September 13th (1831) our paper was able to report that
after being subjected to captious objections and impeded
by vexatious delays unexampled in the annals of Parliament,
after being disputed clause by clause, inch by inch, almost
letter by letter, it had at length passed on the eve of
the coronation of King William IV.
More was needed, averred the East Anglian, than the
reform of the Commons --
'Unless steps are taken to enlighten the working classes
as to their social rights, their social duties and their
personal interests by providing means of instruction for
them, the Reform Bill will be found of very little value.
They must be taught to understand the principles of
supply and demand as regulating the price of labour like
the price of all other commodities'.(17) Later --
'A liberal code of national education is a debt due to
Society at large - due to the poorest classes, due to
the highest'.(18)
The city now went on holiday to celebrate the
Coronation. The theme of Reform was not forgotten. The
illuminations on many whig houses bore the words 'Our patriot King'. Gurney's Bank had a transparency depicting
Britannia supported by Liberty and Justice (The Mercury
identified them as Peace and Hope) watching the sun of
Reform dispel the clouds of despotism. Wilkin and Fletcher
put out 'W crown A' in lamps. A petition was got up in
the city urging the Lords to pass the Bill - a formidable
document - 26 yards long with over 11,000 signatures.
When the Lords rejected it by a sizeable majority there
were riots at Bristol and at Nottingham the Castle was set
on fire. In Norwich a mob surrounded St Peter's to prevent
the ringers raising a peal at the instance of the anti-
reformers. The Mayor, John Harrison Yallop, summonded a
Common Hall to meet at St Andrew's Hall and some 6,000
operatives assembled on the Castle Mound and marched there
carrying banners. Among the inscriptions were - Stand by

the King who stood by you', 'Britons be free', 'A House of
Commons, not an outhouse of Lords', 'Confusion to Bishops
and Borough-mongers'. The last related to the fact that
21 bishops had voted against the Bill, only two for it.
The two were Henry Bathurst, the bishop of Norwich, and
Bishop Maltby of Chichester, a Norwich man, brought up at
the Octagon Chapel. The procession chanted 'God save the
King' as it passed down London Lane, stopping to cheer at
the Mercury Office and at Gurney's Bank. The mood was one
of hope and determination. The East Anglian commented,
   "The rejection of the Bill has not endangered the final
   success of the measure - it must and will be carried".(19)
      The weather too encouraged optimism - "Surely there
never was so serene, so delicious an Autumn". In the Hall
with the Mayor in the chair, Thomas Bignold proposed that
an address be presented to His Majesty expressing the
conviction that Reform was necessary to ensure public tranquility. The resolutions passed, the meeting gave three
cheers for those Peers supporting the Bill, for the King
and his Ministers, nine cheers for Reform and three groans
for the Bishops and quietly dispersed. Though this took
place in October (1831) it was not till the following February that arrangements could be made for the Address to
be presented. Then the Mayor, John Harrison Yallop, his
brother-in-law Nathaniel Bolingbroke, and Robert Grant M.P.
attended the levée and presented the address to the King
who received it graciously and conferred a knighthood on
the Mayor. Citizens opposed to the Bill also got up an
address in the opposite sense which was presented by Lord
Sidmouth.
      Meanwhile conditions of life for the poor remained
lamentable. When the Norfolk Grand Jury met in April
(1832) they were told that commitals to the county gaol
had increased in the year then ended by 30% over those of
the previous year. The East Anglian commented,
   'We may multiply our penal enactments till they are as
   numerous as the sands on the sea-shore but they will not
   suppress crimes against property while hunger, destitution and misery cover the island; .... there are lady
   shop-lifters and rogues in every station of life ....
   still poverty is the most prolific parent of crime.'(20)
      The Bill was reintroduced and in April (1832) passed
its second reading in the Lords. 'The battle is fought,
the victory is won', proclaimed the East Anglian. But it
was not so. The tory majority of Norwich Corporation at
their quarterly Assembly in May voted a petition to the
Lords condemning the Bill as a dangerous and ill-advised
experiment. They prayed their Lordships to reject such a
measure
   'injurious to true liberty, destructive of vested rights
   and opposed to the feelings, habits and interests of all
   Englishmen who are worthy to enjoy the blessings of a
   limited Monarchical Government'.(21)
      At the end of May the Lords once more rejected the
Bill.
   "The tories have done their work; craft, perfidy and
   falsehood are for the hour triumphant .... the will of
   the whole country is set at defiance and its feelings

outraged and insulted".

Once more there was a Common Hall with the Mayor in the chair: once more crowds marched to it in procession. This time there were no banners bearing the King's name – his reluctance to create peers to pass the Bill was resented. 'Britons be free', 'God armeth the patriot', 'Reform and confusion to Bishops and Borough-mongers' were among the slogans. The influence of the Queen against the Bill was resented. Her arms which had adorned Mr Blakely's shop in London Lane as a patroness of Norwich manufactures were taken down and at the meeting Thomas Bignold made an ominous comparison – "Henrietta Maria, Marie Antoinette, Adelaide?" The meeting called on the Commons to withhold all further supplies till the Lords should have passed the Bill.(22) But the King did not in the end desert the cause. His lobbying at length secured the passage of the Bill through the Lords. On June 5th (1832) a Norwich crowd gathered in drenching rain to await the arrival of the Telegraph Coach which brought the news. In July a great celebration was held to mark the victory. St Peter's bells pealed; a cavalcade of a hundred horses was led by R.H. Gurney M.P.; there were bands and banners and floats carrying looms at work and one with a printing press printing verses celebrating Reform which were distributed to the crowds. The procession made its way to the Cricket Ground where an awning had been set up 150 yards long and 30 yards wide. Three tables were laid the length of the tent and the electors sat down to a dinner of cold beef and plum puddings. Dinner was followed by sports and in the evening fireworks on the Castle Mound.

But it was only the whigs who rejoiced. The Lord Lieutenant, Col. John Wodehouse, explaining the meaning of the new political term 'conservatives' said that their principle was to conserve so much of 'the wreck of the Constitution as the revolutionary Reform Bill has still left us'. He then rounded on his opponents, averring:
"Every atheist is a reformer, every deist, everyone who has lost character or respectability, who is poor from whatever cause .... A more zealous reformer than Tom Paine could not exist, and Nockolds, the incendiary, was a reformer".(23)

Politics, however, did not proceed as either side expected. The skirmishing for the first election under the reformed franchise began in July (1832) when the tories adopted Lord Stormont and Sir James Scarlett as their candidates. On the whig side Robert Grant accepted nomination for one of the new Boroughs -- it was said that he had spent £9,000 in Norwich and could afford no more. R.H. Gurney was still in the field and the whig committee chose C.H.B. Ker to run with him. But the radical operatives who had demonstrated so enthusiastically for Reform thought they should have a voice in the choice of a candidate. They apparently sought advice from William Cobbett, who wrote in his Register of August 25th 1832 disparaging Gurney and Ker and recommending William Eagle, 'a learned lawyer .... bent on restoring the working-people to the state in which their fore-fathers lived'. Eagle came to Norwich -- 'A tall, thin, dark, cadaverous

man', said the East Anglian,'looking more like a spiritual
Quixote than an angler for stray votes among the troubled
waters of an election'. He declared himself in favour of
doing away with a standing army, abolishing tithes and
looking into the desirability of taxing machinery.(24)
In the end he seems to have concluded that there was not
sufficient support for his candidacy and so he went home.
His intervention no doubt accounted for the substantial
number of abstensions of former blue-and-white voters when
the poll was taken in December. The election was fought
with all the familiar attributes of Norwich corruption.
The result was not much affected by the new voters whose
support was fairly evenly divided between the two parties.
Simon voted for R.H. Gurney and C.H.B. Ker, the former
having by now regularised his marital position. He had
obtained an Act of Parliament dissolving Mrs Muskett's
former marriage and had wedded her, circumstances which
were the subject of ribald handbills during the election
but seem not to have affected the issue so much as the
defection of the radicals. After three days polling,
Stormont and Scarlett were returned with a substantial
majority. The blue-and-white party raised a howl of
indignation and R.M. Bacon wrote an open letter to the
victors in which he did not hesitate to assert, 'the corrupt means by which your majority was obtained are too
notorious to be any matter of doubt'.
     The city's notorious reputation for corruption
Bacon attributed to party spirit engendered by the frequent
local elections -- for the Common Council, the Sheriff,
the Mayor, and for Aldermen. His remedy, as the East
Anglian described it, was to tear the seal from the perni-
cious Charter of the Corporation and to administer justice
by stipendiary magistrates. The remedy advocated by the
East Anglian was the Secret Ballot. It was said to work
well in America and "until it is instituted here honest
men will be at the mercy of a hired rabble".(25)
     The blue-and-whites appointed a committee with
Sheriff John Cozens in the chair to collect evidence for
a petition against the return of Stormont and Scarlett.
The petition was duly presented in February (1833) and in
April the Committee of the House of Commons found that
Stormont and Scarlett had been duly elected although the
petition against them was not frivolous nor vexatious.
Probably the Committee thought that the performance of the
tories had not been much worse than that of the whigs.
     By this time Wilkin and Fletcher had got tired of
newspaper publishing. Perhaps they had neglected the
'golden pinions to sustain its flight'. The first number
had devoted a quarter of its space to advertisement - that
of April 16th 1833 had less than 15% so occupied. It
carried an announcement that the proprietors had come to
an arrangement with the proprietors of the Bury and Norwich Post to combine the two papers. So the Bury and
Norwich post took over and Simon Wilkin's involvement in
the press came to an end.
     The tradition established was not however lost.
Twelve years later, after Simon had left Norwich, a caucus
of leading dissenters in the city decided to launch yet

another Radical Newspaper with Josiah Fletcher as printer. So the Norfolk News started its career in 1845. Despite early difficulties the paper achieved long-term success, in due course taking over the Mercury and the Chronicle and prospering to this day as the Eastern Counties Newspapers.

REFERENCES

1. Norwich Mercury, 17 January 1829
2. Norwich Mercury, 16 April 1831
3. R. Stedman, Vox Populi
4. East Anglian Herald, 7 December 1830
5. East Anglian Herald, 19 October 1830
6. East Anglian Herald, 5 June 1832
7. East Anglian Herald, 11 December 1832
8. East Anglian Herald, 16 November 1830; 6 December 1831
9. East Anglian Herald, 14 December 1830
10. East Anglian Herald, 21 December 1830
11. East Anglian Herald, 19 April 1831
12. East Anglian Herald, 7 December 1830; Norwich Mercury, 4 December 1830
13. East Anglian Herald, 8 November 1831
14. East Anglian Herald, 9 November 1830
15. Norfolk Chronicle, 26 March 1831
16. East Anglian Herald, 3 May 1831
17. East Anglian Herald, 14 June 1831
18. East Anglian Herald, 19 March 1833
19. East Anglian Herald, 11 October 1831
20. East Anglian Herald, 10 April 1832
21. Norfolk Chronicle, 5 May 1832
22. East Anglian Herald, 15 May 1832
23. East Anglian Herald, 13 November 1832
24. East Anglian Herald, 14 August 1832
25. East Anglian Herald, 25 December 1832

Editor of Sir Thomas Browne's Works

Simon's aspirations to become 'a Literary Character' were not quenched by his misfortunes. About the year 1824, while he was still much involved in the affairs of the Literary Institution, he embarked on the project of publishing a complete edition of Sir Thomas Browne's works. He was acquainted with the Rev. Neville White, brother of Henry Kirk White the poet, who was curate in charge of the church at Great Plumstead near Norwich and through his agency invited Robert Southey to become editor. Southey replied in June 1824 that he could not give the time or care necessary for editing; the best service he could render would be to review the book when published. Having failed to secure Southey as editor, Simon was constrained to undertake the task himself and, said Sir Geoffrey Keynes in 1924,

'the scholarship and painstaking care with which he carried it out have been the delight and admiration of later generations of readers'.(1)

In September 1824 he was in correspondence with the Norwich Antiquary, Samuel Woodward, about details of Browne's *Repertorium* - a series of notes concerning Norwich Cathedral. Woodward supplied him with a drawing shewing the arrangements in the Green-yard on the North side of the Cathedral with its open-air pulpit and galleries to protect the auditors of 'the better sort'.

In 1827 he issued a Prospectus giving an account of the intended work and soliciting the support of subscribers. It was to comprise four volumes at the price of £2.12.6. But the work was still to take a good many years to complete.

He seems first to have concentrated on the most famous of Browne's writings, the *Religio Medici*. He had himself acquired two important manuscript copies of the work. He found a third in the Bodleian and yet another in the British Museum. By October 1829 he was able to sit down and write his preface to this book. His researches enabled him to assign the writing of the *Religio* to the years 1633-1635 when the author was resident at Shibden

Hall near Halifax. Its circulation in manuscript had resulted in the appearance in 1642 of an anonymous and surreptitious edition, which, with the comments and criticisms it attracted, determined Browne to acknowledge it and revise it for the press. His first official edition appeared in 1643. Eight editions had been published in the author's lifetime and six more thereafter, the fourteenth in 1736. Besides these, two Latin editions had been printed in Holland and there were translations into French, German and Dutch and a rumoured one into Italian which Simon had not seen. He had also traced some thirty parallel works from *De Religione Laici* published in London in 1645 to *Religio Militis* in 1827. Simon's version followed the text of the 1643 edition with some amendments from the manuscripts. An edition printed in 1654 had included annotations by T.K., which Simon's research enabled him to attribute to Thomas Keck of the Temple, probably writing in 1644. He printed Keck's annotations and added numerous notes of his own giving comparative texts from various editions and manuscripts and sometimes explanatory quotations from various sources. Joseph Kinghorn's knowledge of Jewish and oriental literature were, no doubt, useful to him: on Browne's speculations about the end of the world, a note quoting from the Talmud bears the initials 'J.K.' and is surely Kinghorn's work.(2) He several times quotes from D'Israeli's *Curiosities of Literature* with illustrations of beliefs in fairies, apparitions and the transmigration of souls. When Browne discusses the scope of salvation through Christ, writing, as Simon says, with a characteristic spirit of charity, he quotes at length and with approval from his friend J.J. Gurney's *Observations on the Religious Peculiarities of the Society of Friends* on the lot of mankind in general: --

"God is their equal judge and compassionate Father: the Son of God .... gave his life a ransom for them all: and .... through the operation of the Holy Spirit a moral sense of right and wrong accompanied with .... quickening and redeeming power is implanted in them universally. Here then, we may perceive grounds of union and brotherly kindness coextensive with the whole world; and .... we shall be disposed neither to think too highly of ourselves, nor to despise others. A feeling of true charity towards our neighbour of whatsoever colour or country will spread in our hearts; and a lively disposition will arise in us to labour for the happiness of the universal family...."(3)

With the completion of the *Religio* Simon found his work not half finished. Many delays occurred in correspondence with people who could assist him 'in hopes of securing advantage to my readers' and he confessed that his plans were often defeated by a spirit of procrastination. One of his correspondents was James Crossley of Manchester who had himself published editions of the *Vulgar Errors* and *Miscellany Tracts* and had intended an edition of the collected works had not Simon forestalled him. Among other things Crossley supplied *'A Fragment on Mummies'*. Unable to trace the original, Simon wrote and asked him where it was to be found. Crossley replied that he had transcribed

it himself but had omitted to note the reference of the
original. Simon printed it under the heading *"Fragment on
Mummies from a copy in the handwriting of J. Crossley Esq."*. It was
proved later to be a product of Crossley's own pen. Crossley was not the only one of his correspondents to indulge
in literary forgery. John Payne Collier, the literary
critic, is said by the Dictionary of National Biography to
have sacrificied an honourable fame won by geniune services
to English literature by a long series of literary frauds.
Happily he does not seem to have perpetrated any in his
correspondence with Simon on Sir Thomas Browne. Among the
correspondents were William Macmichael M.D., Registrar of
the College of Physicians who himself wrote on Sir Thomas
Browne in his *'Lives of the English Physicians'*; Adam Sedgwick,
Woodwardian Professor of Geology at Cambridge; and
R.R. Reinagle R.A. who wrote at length about a picture of
Cleopatra's suicide by the bite of an asp which was said
to have been painted by a contemporary Greek artist. He
gave the history of this curious work of art and even the
chemical analysis of the paints used but "whether it is a
real antique remains still a doubt...".(4) A more important correspondent was Philip Bliss D.C.L., Keeper of the
Archives at Oxford who helped him with the Browne manuscripts in the Bodleian. Bliss found a first edition of
the *Vulgar Errors* with notes written in the margins by Dr
Wren, Dean of Windsor, father of the architect. He had
these copied for Simon who wrote: "In printing nearly the
whole I hope I have enhanced the interest and value of this
edition". Wren's notes involved him in further labours
since they themselves sometimes needed elucidation. Sometimes Browne's scepticism was too much for the good Dean.
When he judges "the set and statary times of paring of
nails and cutting of hair: to be the continuation of an
ancient superstition, Wren is inclined to defend them and
recommends those who would increase the hair to observe
the increasing of the moon especially in Taurus or Cancer,
drawing from Simon the ejaculation "Oh! Mr Dean!" Such
superstitions, he opines,
"will only cease when the ignorance of the lower orders,
through whom they find their way into the nursery, shall
have given place to the general diffusion of knowledge -
especially of religious knowledge".(5)
When Browne wrote of the absence of serpents from
'our neighbour island' the Dean noted that
"in that vast roof of King's College Chappel in Cambridge
.... noe man ever saw a spider, or their webs because it
is all Irish timber."
Simon wrote off to a friend at Cambridge who went
up into the roof and reported that he "could not succeed in
discovering the least appearance of a cobweb, much less a
spider" though he saw many webs in the stone roof beneath.
The Dean wrote that the absence of venemous creatures from
Ireland was a providence of God, "Considering that noe
creature can be worse than the natives themselves", a
sentiment Simon thought not perfectly in keeping with the
character of a Christian minister.(6)
Of all his correspondents Simon was most indebted
to "my kind friend" Thomas Amyot. Thomas who was resident

in London and was Treasurer of the Society of Antiquaries
was the son of a Norwich clockmaker. Simon wrote of him:
"From the commencement of my undertaking to its completion [he] has rendered me in every possible way and with
an unsparing munificence of time, labour and patience,
his own various aid and has ever been prompt to obtain
for me among his extensive acquaintance the help of
others".

Simon collected all the information he could res-
pecting Sir Thomas Browne's family, his literary and
scientific pursuits and habits, his correspondents, his
works and the various criticisms they provoked both at
home and abroad. The reactions proved to have been very
various. One translator had announced him a Protestant;
another a Catholic, while the Holy See had placed his
Religio on the Index Expurgatorius. Samuel Duncon, the
Norwich Quaker, on the basis of statements in the *Religio*
had entertained hopes of winning him to his own opinions,
while German divines represented him as an infidel, almost
an atheist.

Browne's library and manuscripts had passed to his
son and grandson and in January 1710/11 had been sold by
auction in London. With the help of a sale catalogue preserved in the Bodleian Simon compiled a complete list of
his works to insure that he left nothing unpublished. The
far greater part of the collection, he found, had been
purchased by Sir Hans Sloane and had passed to the British
Museum. In 1828 Simon was employing a Mr Chambers to
transcribe the Sloane MSS at the cost of 9d a page. No
part of the work cost more perplexity and labour than the
arrangement of the family correspondence, most of the
letters being without date of year.

It was not till 1835, after he had left Norwich for
London, that Simon came in sight of finishing his labours.
On June 17th 1835 he dated his preface to the *Pseudodoxia
Epidemica or Enquiries into Vulgar and Common Errors* (elsewhere
referred to as *Vulgar Errors*). He believed the book to have
been inspired by Lord Bacon's opinions as to the Use of
Doubts. He traced seven editions and three translations
of this work. Besides Dean Wren's notes already mentioned
he made many more annotations to the *Vulgar Errors*. Alexander
Ross, who had attacked the *Religio* in his *Medicus Medicatus*,
had in 1652 published *Arcana Microcosmi* in which he contro-
verted many of Browne's opinions from the *Vulgar Errors*.
"There is much amusement", says Simon, "to be found in
the volume. He adheres to antiquity 'through thick and
thin'.... but in his very blunders and wrong-headedness
he often shews a quaintness and humour which not a little
atones for them".

So he notes many of Ross's disagreements, for example, when Browne asserted it certainly false that garlic
hinders the loadstone, he wrote,
"I cannot think that the ancient sages would write so
confidently of that they had no experience of ....;
therefore I suppose they had a stronger garlic than is
with us."(7)

When Browne called tears "The uncomfortable attendments of hell" and ventured the opinion that our blessed

Saviour might have laughed as well as wept, Ross suggested
that
"good men find not the uncomfortable attendments in hell
in weeping but rather the comfortable enjoyments of
heaven".
Here he had the support of both the Dean and Simon
who were convinced that Christ never did laugh.(8)
Browne, Simon found, was sometimes mistaken in his
views but the greater number of his errors were those of
universal currency in his days. He was able to shew that
Sir Thomas kept abreast of the discoveries of his times,
pointing out that in the 1672 edition he revised his
remarks on the action of flint on steel to take account of
Dr Hooke's experiments published in 1665.(9)
Simon had readily available the advice of other
Norwich naturalists. He quotes several times 'my old
friend and fellow-citizen Professor Lindley'. Lindley
went to the London markets to identify for him the fruit
sold as 'the forbidden fruit' -- a variety of citrus
decumana, he said. He quotes both Lindley and Sir James
Edward Smith on mistletoe and the mode of its growth.(10)
His own knowledge of entomology enabled him to speak
authoritatively on matters in that range. When Browne
affirms that there is no such insect as the Cicada in
England, he launches into an interesting biographical note:
"About twenty years since, I had the pleasure of adding
this classical and most interesting genus to the British
Fauna. Having about that time engaged Mr Daniel Bydder
(a weaver in Spitalfields and a very enthusiastic entomologist) to collect for me in the New Forest, I received
from him many valuable insects from time to time and at
length to my surprise and great satisfaction a pair of
Cicadae".
The species of this insect proved to be indigenous
and peculiar to this country and it received the appelation
Cicada Anglica. John Curtis was with him at the time and
Simon chides him for not recording the circumstances of
find in his *British Entomology* -
"I should have supposed it might have given him pleasure
to attach to his narrative the name of an old friend from
whom he had received early and valuable assistance ....
At all events he ought to have recorded the name of the
poor man by whose industry and perseverance the discovery
was effected".(11)
In matters of science generally Simon in his notes
quotes from such authorities as the Cuvier brothers, John
Dalton, Erasmus Darwin and Sir Humphrey Davy and from
current papers - the Zoological Journal, the London and
Edinburgh Magazine, the Quarterly Journal of Science and
the Transactions of the Geological Society. When Dr Wren,
commenting on Browne's disquisitions about the Error of
supposing that the elephant has no joints, remarks that
mischief incurred by standing too long (as at studies)
results in the swelling of the legs in old age, he notes
somewhat facetiously:
"Would not Darwin" - he means Erasmus Darwin - "have
said that this swelling was no other than the appetancy
of the leg towards the attainment of the columnar

formation of the elephantine leg - an appetancy excited by the stationary discipline of its studious owner, the Dean?"(12)

Simon thus pokes fun at Darwin but he was plainly acquainted with his foreshadowing of the evolutionary idea - which his grandson would later elaborate. Simon himself accepted the Biblical account of the creation as a matter of faith, but he admitted difficulties and feared that if pursued they might lead to scepticism as he hints in reference to a passage in the *Religio*.

"Whence came the innumerable tribes of human beings, diversified in form, complexion and character which inhabit every continent and island of our globe? Whence the myriads of animals and birds and lesser creatures which everywhere teem in the most astonishing profusion and variety? Who will undertake to make out successive returns of this mighty population, to mark out the progress of its migrations and trace back its genealogies through a succession of 4,000 years up to its cradle, the Ark reposing on the summit of Ararat amidst the silence of universal desolation? It is a question about which so little is known and so much must depend on conjecture that it seems rather calculated for the exercise of ingenuity or even the indulgence of scepticism than likely to lead to the development of truth."(13)

Simon's belief in the divine creation found support in the views of his most admired mentor in the scientific field - Pierre-André Latreille. Latreille, we are told, found it impossible to conceive of the forms of insects and in particular their instinctual behaviour as anything other than the evidence of divine wisdom and design. Furthermore, as he remarked of this view of creation,

"if we are wrong, do not seek to destroy illusions which are useful rather than harmful to society and which make us happy or console us in the difficult pilgrimage of life".(14)

Simon turned to his own family tradition in milling to suggest an elucidation of the Jewish fable of the sabbatical river which flows impetuously all the week but is dry on the Sabbath.

"Only grant the existence of water-corn-mills in the time of the Emperor Titus and the whole is perfectly intelligible. The mills had been at work during the week, keeping up a head of water which had rushed along with a velocity (as Josephus describes it) sufficient to carry with it stones and fragments of rocks. On Sabbath day the miller 'shut down' and let all the water run through by which means the river was laid almost dry".(15)

The question of milling on the Sabbath had certainly engaged Simon's mind when he had been responsible for operations at Taverham. Many millers habitually worked their machinery seven days a week, justifying the practice by the fact that Providence continued to supply the motive power without intermission. Apparently this had been the practice at Taverham up to July 1816 when Simon wrote to Joseph Kinghorn,

"I tell you what will, I am sure, give you pleasure - that Taverham works no more on Sundays".

He made occasional interesting references to current
events and situations. When Browne talks of the possibility of a canal from the Arabian to the Mediterranean
Sea, he comments:
"The long projected intercourse with the East Indies
seems -- under the present enterprising Pacha of Egypt,
to be in a fair way of accomplishment .... The Pacha
has sent to M. Brunel requesting his assistance in
carrying on the great work of improvement in the channel
of the Nile; and one of our British engineers, Mr Gallo-
way, who has the conduct of a railway construction between Cairo and Suez, has been created a Bey of Egypt".
A generation was still to pass before the Suez canal
was actually made.(16)
Some time in 1835 Simon sent to Josiah Fletcher the
manuscripts of the whole work except for his preface, the
Memoirs of Sir Thomas Browne and the correspondence which were
to form the first volume. Thus Volumes II, III, and IV
are dated 1835, Volume I, 1836. Volume II comprised the
Religio and the first four books of *Vulgar Errors*; Volume III
the remaining books of *Vulgar Errors*, the *Garden of Cyprus* ,
Hydrotaphia and the *Brampton Urns*.. The *Garden of Cyprus* has by
general consent, wrote Simon, been regarded as the most
fanciful of Browne's works. In it he considers every work
of art or nature approximating to the form of a quincunx -
the four corner points and centre point of a square -
finding (he quotes Coleridge)
'quincunxes in heaven above, quincunxes in earth below,
quincunxes in the mind of man, quincunxes in tones, in
optic nerves, in roots of trees, in leaves, in everything'.(17)
Simon refers to the Transactions of the Linnean
Society and Reports of the British Association to shew that
the scientists of his day are still interested in 'a quinary distribution in organised nature'. Professor Lindley
has stated, he says, that the most natural groups of plants
of all classes are quinary.(18)
Volume IV contained the *Repertorium*, a *Letter to a Friend*,
Christian Morals, *Miscellany Tracts* and hitherto unpublished
papers. *Christian Morals* Simon thought written on the model
of the Book of Proverbs. He furnished it with notes by
Dr Johnson and some additional quotations from the Sloane
manuscripts. Some of the *Miscellany Tracts* he found were
written as replies to John Evelyn, Sir Nicholas Bacon
and Sir William Dugdale. To the *Tract of Languages* his notes
on the Norfolk dialect and pronunciation are more copious
than the relevant part of the tract, quoting the Rev.
W. Forby's *Vocabulary of East Anglia* and also Miss Gurney of
Northrepps Cottage and Mr Black of the British Museum.(19)
To Sir Thomas's lists of local birds and fishes Simon noted
the common and Latin names and when he gives an account of
whales stranded on Norfolk beaches he brings the account
up to date, telling of one killed at Runton in 1829 about
which Miss Gurney reported,
"It did not look tempting enough to make me bring any of
the meat away but at Northrepps Hall a steak was cooked
and tasted like tender beef".(20)
The preface to the whole edition is dated "Norwich,

28th January 1836" perhaps indicating that Simon came back
to deliver the final instalment of manuscripts to Josiah
Fletcher and to settle the details of printing arrangements.
"Here", he wrote, "I close my labours, content to bespeak
for them the favourable reception of the public in the
quaint language of one of old: - 'If I have done well it
was that which I desired; and if slenderly and meanly it
was that which I could attain unto'".(21)

The worth of the edition did not achieve general
recognition very quickly though Simon received a number of
personal expressions of appreciation. Sir Francis Palgrave
wrote:
"I have looked with great pleasure into your volumes.
You have done the part of an editor nobly".

On the other hand William Stark, who had been concerned with Simon in the Literary Institution, returned
the volumes sent to him saying that Sir Thomas Browne's
subjects were so uninteresting that he would not give half
a crown for them. After ten years the remainder of the
edition was sold to H.G. Bohn who issued a reprint in 1846
and in 1852 a new three volume version.

In July 1837 Robert Southey wrote that it was
settled he should review *Sir Thomas Browne's Works* for the
Quarterly Review. His article never appeared but years
later, after Simon's death, Martin Hood Wilkin purchased
2¼ small quarto pages in Southey's minute hand. Southey
had written:
"This is a handsome edition of one of the most delightful
authors in the English language. None of our prose
writers has ever before been so carefully edited nor is
there one among them upon whom so much diligence could
have been more worthily bestowed. It is also a mark of
local respect of which perhaps there is no other instance
in our country, but which is not less fitting than remarkable, that as Sir Thomas Browne spent the greater
part of his long life in Norwich and is the most eminent
person of which that ancient and still considerable city
can boast, the first compleat collection of his works
should have been printed there and thus elaborately prepared by a townsman, for such the Editor may be called,
although the Author was not a Norwicher by birth. Saints
are commemorated in the Roman Church either on the day
of their birth or of their death -- their first or second
birthdays -- when they were born into the world or out of
it. In like manner the memmorial of any distinguished
person may be found in the history of his native place
or of that in which he fixed his residence, making it his
home by adoption. Sir Thomas Browne was a Londoner, but
in his last Will and Testament styles himself 'of Norwich', there he ended his days and there his monument is
sometimes visited by strangers in respect to the memory
of a great and good man."(22)

Though he never saw Southey's article, Simon happily
lived long enough to receive due recognition of the excellence of his work which has been acclaimed among the
best-edited books in the English tongue.

REFERENCES

1. Geoffrey Keynes, *A Bibliography of Sir Thomas Browne*, Cambridge, 1924. p.233
2. *Sir Thomas Browne's Works*, Bohn's Antiquarian Library, 1852. Vol. II, p.392
3. *Sir Thomas Browne's Works*, Bohn's Antiquarian Library, 1852. Vol. II, p.411
4. *Sir Thomas Browne's Works*, Bohn's Antiquarian Library, 1852. Vol. II, pp.39 - 41
5. *Sir Thomas Browne's Works*, Bohn's Antiquarian Library, 1852. Vol. II, pp.84 and 91
6. *Sir Thomas Browne's Works*, Bohn's Antiquarian Library, 1852. Vol. II, pp.157 and 273
7. *Sir Thomas Browne's Works*, Bohn's Antiquarian Library, 1852. Vol. I, p.136
8. *Sir Thomas Browne's Works*, Bohn's Antiquarian Library, 1852. Vol. II, pp.261 - 262
9. *Sir Thomas Browne's Works*, Bohn's Antiquarian Library, 1852, Vol. I, p.102
10. *Sir Thomas Browne's Works*, Bohn's Antiquarian Library, 1852. Vol. I, p202 and Vol. II, p.210
11. *Sir Thomas Browne's Works*, Bohn's Antiquarian Library, 1852. Vol. II, p.6
12. *Sir Thomas Browne's Works*, Bohn's Antiquarian Library. 1852. Vol. I, p.224
13. *Sir Thomas Browne's Works*, Bohn's Antiquarian Library, 1852. Vol. II, p.353
14. *Dictionary of Scientific Biography*
15. *Sir Thomas Browne's Works*, Bohn's Antiquarian Library, 1852. Vol. II, p.282
16. *Sir Thomas Browne's Works*, Bohn's Antiquarian Library, 1852. Vol. II, p.176
17. *Sir Thomas Browne's Works*, Bohn's Antiquarian Library, 1852. Vol. II, p.492
18. *Sir Thomas Browne's Works*, Bohn's Antiquarian Library, 1852, Vol. II, pp.554 - 6
19. *Sir Thomas Browne's Works*, Bohn's Antiquarian Library, 1852. Vol. III, pp.233 - 8
20. *Sir Thomas Browne's Works*, Bohn's Antiquarian Library, 1852. Vol. III, p.324
21. *Sir Thomas Browne's Works*, Bohn's Antiquarian Library. 1852. Vol. I, pp.v - viii
22. Keynes, op. cit. p.341

Church member

We have seen that at an early age Simon became a
member of the Baptist church meeting in St Mary's and
commonly known by that name. He was active in the affairs
of the church and his life was often influenced by his
relationship to his fellow-members. He took a particular
interest in the music of the church. Long ago (in 1810)
he had been involved in organising the choir and in June
1829 he was busy with a reorganisation. He wrote to
Joseph Kinghorn:
"I am requested by some of our friends at St Mary's to
write to you to ask your consent to an alteration of the
pulpit there in order to provide room for a singing seat:
viz to place the pulpit with a flat back against the wall
and to construct seats for singers in the centre in front
of the pulpit. At the meeting held in consequence of
your notice a subscription list was opened and Mr David,
Mr Pratt and myself appointed a committee to form the
choir with Mr Hill and to form anew the collection of
Hymn tunes under the general principal of preference for
simple and aversion to fugue tunes.
The committee has struck out about 60 tunes - and
our present appointments to the new choir under the
premiership of Mr Hill are as follows:
    Mr Hill, leader
    Mr Widdows Senr. (on pension)
    Mr Barwick - to be exceedingly drilled
    Mr Sadler Junr, a tenor
    Mr Pratt
    Mr Sadler (the Senr. a Bass)
These with the Boys are to be invited to hold their
first meeting for practice in my drawing room on Thursday
evg at seven."[1]
John Hill who was to lead the choir was sometime
conductor of the Norwich Choral Society and later to be co-
editor with his son of the *Norwich Tune Book* published in 1844
containing 250 hymn-tunes suitable for divine worship.
The 'family' relationship of the members of 'St
Mary's' one to another was remarkable. It was emphasised
by Joseph Kinghorn who said to his church after his father
died in 1822,
"I am now loosened from every earthly tie and have no
other care but you. Henceforth you, the members of this
church, shall be my brother and my sister, my father and

my mother"(2)
    Simon's special relationship to Joseph Kinghorn
meant that he was at the heart of church affairs and
prominent among his fellow members. We shall therefore
look at some of those with whom he associated.
    The Senior Deacon of the church was Thomas Hawkins,
father of Simon's school-fellows William and Anne Hawkins.
He was a grocer and lived with Martha his wife and a numerous family over his shop at the corner of Tombland and
Queen Street, facing the Ethelbert Gate into the Cathedral
Close. His church connections helped him in his business
and assisted him to buy dried fruit in Hull and both butter
and lead shot in Newcastle, all which commodities were
shipped coastwise via Yarmouth. He was already in charge
of church affairs in 1789 when he welcomed Joseph Kinghorn
at his first coming here. He arranged for preachers to
fill the pulpit at St Mary's during Kinghorn's absences
and at worship himself gave out the hymns from the box
under the pulpit. He was Supervisor of the 'Society held
in the Baptist Chapel in the parish of St Mary's for the
mutual Benefit of its Members in the time of Sickness and
Death', and invested the proceeds of the shilling a month
collected from the contributors who were the poorer members
of the congregation. In his early days he had been active
in radical politics and, evading the operation of the Test
Act, a member of the Common Council. Towards the end of
his life (he died in 1841) he no longer bothered to keep
up with the times - it is said that he was the last man in
Norwich to wear a pigtail, though there are other claimants
for this distinction.
    For some years Thomas Hawkins had carried the re-
sponsibilities of the diaconate alone when in 1813 the
church appointed James Cozens as his colleague and in 1822
he handed over to Cozens the main duties of the office.
James Cozens, who was Simon's senior by some twenty years,
came of a family deeply involved in the radical politics
of Norwich. His brother John had been a leading 'Jacobin'
in the 1790s as was Jonathon Davey who had married his
sister Emma. John and Jonathon were active members of St
Clement's Baptist Church under the pastorate of the Rev.
Mark Wilks, a most enthusiastic supporter of the French Revolution. The fact that James chose St Mary's rather than
St Clement's perhaps suggests that he was not such an ardent
politician.
    Many of the church families were connected by mar-
riage. James Cozens married Ruth, sister of another member,
Jeremiah Colman, who in his turn was married to a sister of
Thomas Theobald, who again married another of the Colman
sisters. Thomas and Jeremiah had been baptized together by
Kinghorn in 1806. In earlier years Thomas had been very
intimate with Kinghorn for whom he bought books when in
Germany on business. In 1811 he contributed £100 to the
building of the new chapel. Jeremiah gave £50, an indi-
cation of their relative prosperity at the time. Thomas
Theobald seems to have been a successful trader in Norwich
stuffs and he was also much.interested in agriculture; the
diary he kept for many years is concerned chiefly with the
weather, the harvests and the seasonal variations of flowers

and foliage. In July 1828 he wrote a long letter to Kinghorn deploring the unfavourable alteration in the latter's
appearance in regard to health, which he attributed to his
devoting to controversial matters time which ought to have
been given to relaxation. He recommended him to stop writing new sermons and to use old ones from his extensive and
valuable hoard. It is unlikely that this advice was followed. Not long after, as we shall see, he was himself to
cause some anxiety to his pastor.

Jeremiah Colman came of a farming family associated
with Great Ellingham Baptist Church. He was a miller and
two years after Simon became interested in the Taverham
water-mill he acquired that at Stoke-Holy-Cross. Whereas
Simon failed in paper-making, Jeremiah made mustard and
prospered. Having no children of their own he and his wife
adopted and brought up a nephew, James Colman, who, shortly
after coming of age was taken into partnership (in 1823) to
form the firm of J. & J. Colman. Both Jeremiah and James
became pillars of St Mary's, driving up from Stoke in a gig
which was put up at the Woolpack in St George's during
services. James, who was Simon's junior by 11 years, like
him took a special interest in the church's music.

Another member of the older generation was John
Sherren Brewer, a schoolmaster. He came from Kent and
joined St Mary's in 1812, having married a child of the
church, Elizabeth Kitton. Their family pew was occupied
by an increasing number of children - the St Mary's register records the births of nine from John Sherren junior
in 1809 to Rachel in 1824, in which year her father moved
his school from the cramped quarters of Calvert Street to
Eaton, a mile out of the city on the Newmarket turnpike.
He had, he said in his prospectus, tried to improve the
character of his school by studying new developments in
public education. At Eaton the salubrity of the air, the
extensiveness of ground appropriated for amusement, the
complete separation from casual intercourse and the facility for conveyance by coaches were rarely equalled. His
buildings were to be ventilated by an apparatus guaranteed
to keep the air pure and temperate at all seasons. His
system of discipline was so correct as to render it impossible for a pupil to be absent more than ten minutes
without detection or to avoid by any artifice the performance of appointed duties. The school occasionally produced
a magazine of essays and verses - *"Horae Feriatae"* - which
Simon printed for them in 1825 and again in 1828.

J.S. Brewer was learned in the classics and in Hebrew which endeared him to Joseph Kinghorn who counted him
among his most intimate friends.

Several of the Brewer children inherited their
father's academic abilities. John Sherren junior became an
eminent historian and was editor of the *Calender of State
Papers of the reign of Henry VIII*; William a Surgeon and Member
of Parliament for Colchester; Robert Kitton - named after
his mother's father - a Doctor of Music and Baptist Minister; two of the daughters ran a Girl's School in Norwich;
but the best known was Ebenezer Cobham, author of the
famous *Dictionary of Phrase and Fable*. Already in 1831 before
going up to Trinity Hall, he was amassing the information

which he used in the Dictionary. In that year he wrote in the album of another child of the church "Verses to Miss M.A. Smith", replete with classical allusions.

Mary Smith was daughter of Joseph Smith and his wife Catherine (née De Carle) a descendant of Huguenot refugees. They lived in a commodious house opposite St Saviour's church where they kept a chemist's shop. Catherine was a woman of character, brought up to entertain a due sense of her position. At the age of eight she had embroidered on her sampler verses thanking her parents for bestowing on her the means of learning and begging to be allowed still to pursue "those golden arts the vulgar never knew". In 1821 when her husband died at the age of 35 she took charge of the chemist's shop and carried it on till her eldest son Joseph De Carle Smith was ready, after apprenticeship to herself and further training in London, to enter into partnership with her. Joseph was later to be a deacon of the church and Mayor of the city.

We have already met with Thomas Bignold helping Simon at the time of his bankruptcy. He was three years older than Simon and brought up an Anglican, son of Thomas Bignold, the redoubtable founder of the Norwich Union Insurance Societies. In 1809 he had gone to London for legal training with Messrs. Bleasdale in New Inn. Here he met Edward Bickersteth, described as 'a terrible methodist'. A warm friendship sprang up between the two as a result of which Bickersteth came to Norwich, married Thomas's sister and entered into partnership with his brother-in-law as an attorney. They determined moreover to conduct their business on 'strictly religious principles'. Their active pursuit of religion brought them into touch with Joseph Kinghorn. Bignold and his wife embraced Baptist views and were baptised at St Mary's in June 1815; Bickersteth on the other hand secured Orders in the Anglican Church and became Secretary of the Church Missionary Society, continuing to correspond with Kinghorn whose advice he evidently valued. After Bickersteth had left him, Thomas Bignold found a new partner in Simon's brother-in-law Thomas Brightwell. In politics Thomas Bignold was nearly as active on the whig side as his brother Samuel was among the tories and in the excitements leading up to the Reform Act of 1832 the two were leading speakers for and against the reform of Parliament though at the same time Thomas was supporting his brother's candidacy for the Governor of the Court of Guardians.

These known people were of course a small minority of the congregation at St Mary's. The majority is inevitably anonymous though occasionally the veil is lifted. A little bundle of letters in Kinghorn's correspondence told how two of his humbler members, Edward Goose, a tailor, and his wife were thrown into deep distress by their son Jacob running away to join the army. They went to Kinghorn who called on the Mayor, John Harrison Yallop, who wrote to the Adjutant General as to the boy's whereabouts. A reply came, dated from Horse Guards, December 6th 1815, with the information that Jacob was with the 85th regiment at Hythe. His parents were thus enabled to correspond with the runaway and a few weeks later received a letter from him

telling that he was in good health and spirits and aboard
the Valiant Ship 'Isle of Wight'.(3)   Edward Goose sub
scribed his 1/- a month to the St Mary's Mutual Benefit
Society and on a number of occasions drew benefits.
Another member whose name only comes to light because of
misfortune was William Beare, who was employed as a clerk
by Starling Day, a banker and sometime Mayor.   When he
died of typhus fever in 1832 he left a wife and eleven
children in a state of destitution.   A fund was opened for
their relief to which Simon subscribed £5 as did Joseph
Kinghorn, Thomas Hawkins, James Cozens, John Culley, Jeremiah Colman and Thomas Bignold among others.(4)

In those days the multiplicity of clubs and societies which form the activities of a twentieth century
church were unknown.   Apart from the Church Meeting which
governed their affairs, the only activity of the church
was public worship.   The conduct of worship at St Mary's
was of a high order - Simon often drew unfavourable comparisons when he had occasion to attend worship away from
home.   Kinghorn's preaching, we are told, reflected his
immense range of reading and study while acquaintance with
mathematics, philosophy, mechanics and trades of various
kinds enabled him to draw apt comparisons to illustrate
his subjects.   Of his preaching Simon's niece, Cecilia
Lucy Brightwell, wrote:
"He fixed the attention of his hearers by the peculiar
manner in which he treated his subject.   One of his
favourite methods was to bring forward some imaginary
opponent.   'Here starts up an objector' he would say and
then would proceed to state the arguments generally used.
.... This was done with much vigour and spirit and I
well remember how satisfactory it was to see the adversary dislodged and his stronghold taken by storm.   In
the practical application of his subject he especially
excelled, ... ever pointing to Christ and Him crucified.
His impressive manner and appearance, his frequent emotion
often testified by his faltering voice and gathering
tears enlisted the sympathy of his auditors and imparted
to his ministrations a special power.   What he said left
an abiding impression".(5)
Kinghorn's administration of the sacraments (he
would have said ordinances) was impressive.   Years later
Simon remembered the baptisms - his commanding figure
standing at the water's edge to address the candidates
before leading them into the pool.   A witness of his conduct of the Lord's Supper wrote:
"There was a pause before the commencement of the service
till all minds were hushed, the thoughts composed and
stillness reigned.   Even at the commencement of the
ordinance his feelings seemed to have more than usual
animation and joy and towards the close .... he often
seemed to me to be living in a triumph of expectation
and joy which wrapped his soul and bore him and those
around him for the present above all earthly things to
the realisation of a degree of bliss known but there....
After administering the bread and wine to others he continued when partaking of it himself some little time in
perfect quiet and meditation; and when he opened the

93

hymn-book, placed it on one of the cups, and after some words of exhortation and comfort, read in a manner which uttered his whole soul some favourite hymn, the thrill of divine love and joy which it seemed to communicate had an effect on me which I cannot but feel among my deepest impressions of the blessedness of such a hope".(6)

The church also provided its members with a window on the distant world. From the time that William Carey went to India in 1793 - in the face of strong opposition from the East India Company and the establishment generally - its members received reports from overseas missionaries giving them a view of far off peoples and events quite different from that available to those who could read the newspapers. In the 1820s they forged personal links with the foreign field. Joshua Tinson spent some time here under the tuition of Joseph Kinghorn before going to Jamaica in 1822, while Andrew Leslie occupied the St Mary's pulpit for several months while Kinghorn was in Scotland and made many friends in the congregation before he made the six-months journey to Calcutta. These two corresponded with Kinghorn and with other members of the church. Tinson's complaints of the constant hostility of the Jamaica planters to missionary work, reinforced by a personal visit from his colleague William Knibb, are reflected in Simon's annotation to Sir Thomas Browne's comment on the 'prophecy' "Africa shall no more sell out their blacks". He wrote: "The abolition of the slave trade and the American efforts to colonize and evangelise Africa may be regarded as two important steps towards the fulfilment of this prophecy. One measure remains to be adopted - the emancipation of the slaves in the West Indies: - a measure of equity which, if not carried by legislation, will ere long be effected by means far less desirable".(7)

Simon dated his note December 1832 - by the time the book was published, parliament had abolished slavery in the British Empire.

Interest in the Baptist Irish Society also made a link with that unhappy island. An appeal made in the summer of 1831 to all the churches to contribute to the relief of the famine in Ireland was reinforced at St Mary's by a letter from the Society's agent, the Rev. J. Allen, copied to Joseph Kinghorn, giving a lurid account of the situation. Hundreds, Allen said, must inevitably die. He was doing what he could to distribute aid to the 200 families connected with the Society's schools and would need £50 - £60 a week for the next five weeks to keep up his programme. Suits of clothes were also wanted but these would be useless without money. As a result the St Mary's congregation raised £115, substantially more than any other church in the city.(8)

In 1830 the even tenor of church life was disturbed by a dispute between two members, Thomas Theobald and John Darken. The two had been in partnership in an unsuccessful enterprise in iron-founding and Theobald charged Darken with underhand conduct in the matter. The church appointed a committee to investigate; its members included Simon, his father-in-law John Culley and Jeremiah Colman who was Theobald's brother-in-law. The committee found that the

charges were without foundation. Thomas Theobald refused to withdraw them and therefore left the church, worshiping thenceforth at the Old Meeting where his memorial tablet may still be seen. Doubtless Joseph Kinghorn was saddened by this defection. Perhaps he remembered that when the Theobald family first came to St Mary's nearly forty years before he had commented in a letter to his father:
"They are not so likely to be pleasing members as some others (God having some awkward sheep in His Fold)".

REFERENCES

1. Wilkin Papers, 127. S.W. to J.K. 15 June 1829
2. M.H. Wilkin, op. cit. p.381
3. C.B.J. notes 20/21
4. Norwich Mercury, 14 January 1832
5. C.L. Brightwell, *Memorials of the Life of Mr Brightwell* p.39
6. M.H. Wilkin, op. cit. p.447
7. *Sir Thomas Browne's Works*, Bohn edition 1852.
   Vol. III, p.294
8. East Anglian Herald, 28 June & 5 July 1831

Last years in Norwich

In 1831 the Asiatic Cholera reached England. Towards the end of the year its spread caused growing anxiety. Norwich manufacturers attributed the stagnation of their trade to the panic resultant from it in London and elsewhere. On August 11th 1832 the Norwich Mercury reported thirty cases in the city and seven deaths. In the following weeks the death-toll mounted. Just at this time William Knibb, the Jamaica missionary, came to Norwich to campaign against slavery. He had recently returned from the island after narrowly escaping death at the hands of the slave-owners. On Saturday August 25th Kinghorn wrote on his behalf to John Williams, the Baptist Minister at Dereham, about plans for Knibb's visit to that town the following week. That same day Kinghorn was struck down by a fever. Next morning there was no question of his undertaking his normal Sunday duties. When his congregation assembled for morning worship they were surprised to see William Knibb enter the pulpit and alarmed to learn the reason for this substitution. During the week Kinghorn's fever grew worse. No doubt Simon was involved in measures to deal with the situation. It was surely he who mobilised the doctors for we are told that three were in attendance - Mr Dalrymple and Dr Wright, respectively the city's leading surgeon and leading physician, and Dr Ash. Despite their efforts the patient grew weeker and on Saturday evening September 1st passed away. Thomas Theobald wrote in his journal;
"The cholera having been prevalent at Norwich for more than a fortnight, his [Kinghorn's] attack which nearly ressembled it was supposed to be cholera."
Years later Simon recollected:
"When first, after his departure I entered his study and sat down in his large arm-chair, I looked sorrowfully around upon the books which filled his shelves and I found, just as he had left them, a mass of papers and letters at the end of his table; and opposite to his chair his writing materials, his commonplace book and some unanswered and unfinished letters. It seemed to me as if he had just quitted the apartment and might re-enter the next moment with his tall figure and ample morning gown to give me again his kindly and cordial welcome, as oft times before."
In the East Anglian Herald Simon published the

following obituary, which was copied by the two other
Norwich papers:
"Seldom does it fall to the lot of a public journalist
to announce a bereavement which will be more deeply felt
and more widely lamented .... His natural qualities
were extraordinary sagacity, elasticity and energy of
mind.
His moral qualities were simplicity and integrity
of heart, an entire devotedness to the duties of his
calling, an unabating regard for the claims of affection
and friendship, an ardent and ever-growing piety and a
lively and constant sympathy with the joys and sorrows
of his fellow men. His literary qualities were unwearied
diligence, deep and erudite enquiry, especially into all
subjects connected with theology and moral philosophy....
His social qualities were a kind and graceful
courteousness, a readiness to communicate from the stores
of his knowledge with a familiarity calculated both to
instruct and to encourage his companions and especially
the young; with a lively spirit and a native humour which
enabled him to enjoy and to diffuse the pleasures of
society ...."
With Kinghorn's death at the age of 66 an irreplace-
able loss seemed to be suffered by Norwich society. A
country clergyman was reported to have said, 'If half Norwich had died the loss would not have been so much felt.'
His own church was most directly affected. As Dr Stoughton
wrote,
'Kinghorn was almost worshipped by his congregation, who
regarded him as a sage and deemed it a high honour to
receive him into their houses.'(1)
James Cozens, the acting senior deacon at St Mary's,
was left in charge of the church's affairs. The first
action taken to meet the situation was the appointment of
three more deacons to work with him - Jeremiah Colman,
Simon Wilkin and John Gooderson. Simon and Jeremiah were
in many ways contrasting characters; Jeremiah robust,
jovial and extrovert, a successful man of business and
active in public affairs - he was later to be Sheriff and
the Mayor of the city - Simon introspective, liable to
moods of depression, devoted to science and literature and
often ill at ease in society. Of John Gooderson we know
little. He had joined the church in 1813 and was a draper
with a shop in the marketplace.
The first concern of the new diaconate was to find
a minister for the church. On the second Sunday in January
1833 the pulpit was taken by William Brock, a third year
student at the Stepney Academy, the institution which had
tried to secure Kinghorn as its first Principal. The
church fell for him at once. He preached again in February
when the deacons discussed with him the possibility of his
settling at Norwich and offered to reduce the usual probationary period (which in Kinghorn's case had been nearly a
year) to two months. Brock was at the same time being
pressed by a London church to accept their pastorate. The
perplexities arising from these invitations together with
the necessity of keeping abreast of his college work were
too much for the young man. His health gave way and he

went home to Devonshire to recuperate. So anxious were
the St Mary's deacons to secure his services that they sent
John Gooderson to Devon to express their sympathy and to
offer him the pastorate without any probationary period at
all. This ploy had the desired result -- Brock agreed to
come. While they were awaiting their new minister the
church felt able to exert its influence in public affairs.
Acting in concert with the Independents at Prince's Street
Chapel they got up a petition against Sunday trading which
was presented to the House of Lords by Lord Suffield in
March (1833).

Brock came to Norwich in May and on the last day of
the month met the deacons of St Mary's at James Cozens'
house and accepted the offer of the pastorate. He was duly
ordained in July when the President of Stepney College and
local Baptist and Independent ministers took part in the
ceremony as did William Hawkins, Simon's old schoolfellow
who was now a minister at Derby where he had tutored Brock
before his admission to Stepney.(2) Years afterwards Simon
recollected that Hawkins had preached an excellent sermon
on this occasion. Simon seems to have shared the spirit
of enthusiasm for the new young minister. He had been
present at the small meeting on May 31st when the sensitive
Brock would surely have noted any suspicion of coolness.
Once Brock was settled in Norwich we are told that it was
no uncommon thing for him to receive in the early part of
the week a letter from Simon - and sometimes from other
hearers - expressing some difference of opinion on his
Sunday sermons and founding his representations on the
original Greek or Hebrew scriptures which would be quoted
at length. These communications were not resented for
Brock had been advised before he came to Norwich to court
and profit by Simon's criticism.(3)

Early in 1834 Brock was afflicted with an infection
of the throat. His doctor decreed a month's silence but
this did not mend matters. Brock felt that there was no
course open to him but to resign. His deacons however told
him this would be premature and sent him home to Devon.
After another month had elapsed without a cure they wrote
directing him to consult the most eminent physician in
reach. When the physician ordered a further three months
treatment they sent him a present of £50 for his expenses.
Further they sent Jeremiah Colman to see him and report on
his progress. Jeremiah was pleased with what he saw and
told the church they might expect all to be well at the end
of the three months, as indeed it was.(4)

These vicissitudes naturally bound the church and
their pastor closer to one another in mutual regard but
Simon soon began to diverge from the direction in which
William Brock was leading. All had held Joseph Kinghorn
in sincere veneration: no one would have dreamed of quest-
ioning his principles or even his prejudices. Now that he
was gone the majority were ready to respond to a new leader-
ship even if it involved a change of direction. With Simon
the case was otherwise. Of all his circle Simon had been
nearest to Kinghorn in his lifetime. In earlier days he
had not hesitated frankly to differ from his old guardian.
The differences had not in any way impaired their relation-

ship but time had sometimes proved the wisdom of Kinghorn's
views. Now that Kinghorn was gone his opinions could no
longer be disputed. More and more Simon came to regard
them as holy writ.

The Baptist churches were divided on the question
as to whether it was right to admit Christians who had not
been baptised on profession of their faith to the Communion
of the Lord's Supper. Kinghorn had been the champion of
the closed Communion table, conducting a long controversy
in books and pamphlets against the redoubtable Robert Hall,
the exponent of the Open Table. From the first Brock had
made it clear that he espoused Hall's opinion. There was
no immediate change but the style of proceedings altered.
Brock was more inclined than his predecessor to involve
himself in political affairs. It was said of him that he
preached from the Bible and the Times newspaper.

Simon had already demonstrated how touchy he was in
matters concerning the memory of his late friend and mentor. A Norwich printer, J.M. Johnson, had been minded to
draw and publish a portrait of the late Joseph Kinghorn.
Knowing that Simon possessed a miniature portrait he went
to the shop of Wilkin and Fletcher and asked if he could
borrow it. Simon being out, Josiah Fletcher let him see
the portrait but would not permit him to borrow it. When
Simon heard what had happened he called on Johnson and 'in
an angry tone' requested to see his drawing which he declared was 'a libel on his late friend'. Johnson wrote to
the papers publicly rebuking him --
"I have only to express my regret that Mr Wilkin should
have so widely departed from the line of conduct which
it was the daily concern of his late friend to inculate,
and which every liberal and upright mind desires to
exemplify."

Simon proceeded to have an engraving of his miniature made by William Bond. Bond's engraving is certainly
a smoother and more elegant picture than Johnson's litho-
graph, though the latter has perhaps more feeling and
character. Josiah Fletcher thought well of it and asked
Johnson to reserve the original for him.(5) Simon published Bond's engraving in October (1833) and announced
that he proposed a Memoir of Mr Kinghorn with selections
from his correspondence as soon as an adequate number of
subscriptions were obtained. In fact the memoir was not
published till twenty years later when Simon's son Martin
undertook it. Presently Simon was engaged in cataloguing
Kinghorn's library of 4,000 volumes with a view to their
sale.

Changes were happening in other spheres of Simon's
interest. The Museum was outgrowing the premises he let
to it and the committee wanted to cancel the lease and move
elsewhere. In the Spring of 1833 they finalised their
plans for a move and the foundation stone of a new building
in Exchange Street to house their collections was laid at
the end of May.

Impending changes in the city's affairs too cast
their shadows before them. In November (1833) two of the
Municipal Commissioners arrived in Norwich to investigate
the affairs of the Corporation. The King had appointed the

Commission at the request of the reformed House of Commons. The Norwich Sheriffs declined to attend or to allow their officers to give evidence before the Commissioners on the grounds that their Commission had been issued by virtue of the Royal Prerogative alone, a process unknown to the law of England and eminently hostile to public liberty. The Mayor, Samuel Bignold, was more guarded than the Sheriffs. Though doubtful as to the validity of the Commission he allowed the City's charters to be produced and housed the Commissioners in the Guildhall where they took evidence from numerous citizens who were willing to tell tales about their experience of the operation of the municipal machinery. For 21 days the Commissioners were in session. The revelations made to them were the talk of Norwich. If we may believe what was told them the elections of Aldermen seem to have produced the worst practices. Once elected an Alderman enjoyed his status and the privilege and patronage that went with it for the rest of his life and some aspirants were prepared to go to great lengths to secure election. Four witnesses gave their account of a formidable instance of kidnapping and 'cooping' by the orange-and-purple supporters of John Angell, a currier, who was elected Alderman in 1827. Two of the witnesses had been taken by force in Ber Street and dragged to the Butcher's Arms; another had been hustled into the Bell and yet another called there on pretext of business. With one or two others they had been taken by coach under guard to the village of Panxworth where they had been locked up at the Lion. Later they were removed to Ranworth and put on board a wherry. They were given rum mixed with laudanum but one of them, Robert Alden, refusing to drink it remained sober and when the wherry came near the bank succeeded in jumping ashore and escaping. He borrowed a horse and gig and got back to Norwich in time to vote for Angell's opponent. The wherry sailed off to Horsey Mere, pursued by another chartered by the blue-and-whites to rescue the prisoners. The second wherryman gave evidence that he had overtaken his quarry at Acle Bridge but the guards on duty were armed with scythes and he had not dared attempt a boarding. When the election was safely over the prisoners were released at Ranworth and left to find their way home. The wherry-owner also gave evidence that he had supplied beer, meat, bread and tobacco to the prisoners and had sent in a bill for £75 to the orange-and-purple party who had promised to be accountable for 'Friends of Mr Angell's taking refreshment at his house' -- he had only been paid £35! Another witness said that the whole city had been in a state of disorder during this election so that no active partisan on either side was safe. The orange-and-purples had even been bold enough to 'coop' a number of whig voters in a warehouse belonging to one of their opponents, Nathaniel Bolingbroke, but he discovered it and had them released.

Many witnesses recounted -- almost boasted of -- the amounts they had paid for votes on various occasions. One put down the bribery which was acknowledged to have taken place in the 1832 election to the new franchise -- whereas in the past the parties had spent money in bringing in 'out-voters', freemen living in London or the country, as these had lost their qualification to vote, the money which would have been spent on them was now available to buy votes.(6)

R.M. Bacon of the Norwich Mercury, who had been much concerned about corrupt practices since the blue-and-whites lost the 1832 election, reported the lurid details of the evidence and concluded that more had been proved than he, as editor, had ever advanced -- 'not one solitary atom of respect was left to the Corporation, more than belonged to the Whifflers' (attendants on the Mayor's procession) 'or to Snap' (the canvass dragon). The Recorder of Norwich, Isaac Preston, took strong exception to Bacon's strictures. Addressing the Grand Jury, he called attention to the character of the witnesses, some of them bankrupts, others who had openly declared themselves guilty of the foulest corruption. He impugned the evidence taken, the lack of cross-examination and the failure to check one witness's evidence against another's. Attacking Bacon he said,

"I do not envy the individual who after 50 years acquaintance can speak thus of his native city", but (regretfully), "I know that the world at large is in a great degree governed by the Press".(7)

The Corporation too at a special assembly held on January 9th (1834) registered their protest against the proceedings of the Commissioners, expressing regret and disapproval at the course of the examination and resolving to make common cause with other Corporations to preserve their ancient Charters, Franchises and Liberties.

When all allowances have been made for exaggeration and party spirit, there can be no doubt that the evidence given proved the need for reform of the Corporation, a reform which was to be effected two years later by the Municipal Corporations Act.

Weak as were the policing arrangements under the old regime, they were not wholly ineffective. One night in March (1834) the Watchman found the door of Wilkin and Fletcher's shop unfastened. Josiah Fletcher was called down and found the till rifled. He was smart enough to spot the thief escaping over the roof of the back premises. With the help of a neighbour Josiah tracked him to a nearby outhouse, recovered the missing cash and handed over the burglar to justice.(8)

By now it seems that Simon was anxious to caste off from his moorings and leave the city. Such a change in his intentions is not easily accounted for at a time when the population was so stable and his own roots so well-established in Norwich soil. We can only conjecture that he was unable to reconcile himself to life in Norwich without the guiding light of Joseph Kinghorn's wisdom and the support of his established reputation. In his youth he had held radical views - he could not drink the King's health 'sine grimacibus' - and he had always been on the side of Reform. But those who strive for change and enjoy the battle do not necessarily appreciate the consequences when the battle has been won. He was unwilling to adjust himself to the new style in the church at St Mary's.

Probably he was not enamoured of the impending changes in
the government of the city, though those changes were
shortly to bring some of his associates into positions of
prominence which had seldom been enjoyed by dissenters
under the old order -- his brother-in-law Thomas Brightwell
would be Mayor in 1837 and his fellow-deacon Jeremiah Colman some years later.

On August 12th (1834) he dissolved his partnership
with Josiah Fletcher, writing to the Mercury:
"I have relinquished my business in this city to my
former apprentice and late partner Mr Fletcher. But I
cannot allow the opportunity to pass by without some
expression of my own feelings. Sixteen years have passed
away since I appealed to the sympathy of the public for
support in my efforts to regain the independence of which
misfortune had deprived me on the very threshold of life.

In retiring from business I now beg to acknowledge
and shall ever gratefully remember the readiness with
which my appeal was answered and especially the feelings
of personal respect and kindness which have uniformly
been evinced towards me during so long a period. Of
those feelings I am anxious once more to avail myself on
behalf of my successor, for whom I earnestly entreat that
patronage and support which I am sure his character will
justify, and trust his exertions will endeavour to de-
serve. I am respectfully, S. Wilkin."(9)

Simon was still librarian to the Norfolk and Norwich
Literary Institution. He wrote to them in October (1834)
complaining that whereas they paid him £50 a year, he was
obliged to pay an assistant at £1 a week and so was £2 out
of pocket. He asked them to make this up and also to remit
his annual subscription. The subscription was remitted,
with a rider that he would no longer be eligible to be a
member of the committee; the matter of the £2 they decided
to pass over in silence.

Before the Wilkins left Norwich Josiah Fletcher
informed them that he was engaged to be married to Sarah
Williams of Camberwell. He arranged to hire from Simon the
furniture in the Haymarket house till next Ladyday so that
his bride, when she came, could purchase furniture to her
own taste. On November 7th 1834 he wrote to Sarah telling
her that Mr and Mrs Wilkin were to leave Norwich on Monday
November 10th with the three children and a nursemaid by
coach.(10)

So Simon's life in Norwich came to an end. Henceforth his address was Cossey Cottage, Hampstead.

REFERENCES

1. Dr John Stoughton. *History of Religion in England*. 1884
   Vol. VII p.267
2. C.M. Birrell. *Life of William Brock*. 1878, p.54
3. C.M. Birrell. *Life of William Brock*.   p.92
4. C.M. Birrell. *Life of William Brock*.   p.105
5. Norwich Mercury, 19 January 1833
6. *A Digest of Evidence taken before two of His Majesty's Municipal
   Corporation Commissioners at the Guildhall in the City of Norwich*. 1834

7. Norwich Mercury, 4 January 1834
8. Norwich Mercury, 22 March 1834
9. Norwich Mercury, 16 August 1834
10. Letter in the possession of Mrs Jill Paine,
    a descendent of Josiah Fletcher

Epilogue

With his departure in November 1834 Simon's Norwich career ended. When his son, Martin Hood Wilkin, came to write the notice on his father for the *Dictionary of National Biography* he recorded that 'in the latter part of his life he removed to London, residing at Hampstead'. In truth Simon was forty four years old at the time of the move and was to live twenty eight years longer. But the achievements of his life belonged to the Norwich years. Apart from the publication of his edition of *Sir Thomas Browne's Works* in 1836 - the major part of the work having been done while he was in Norwich - Martin mentions only the provision of an introductory chapter to *'Joseph Kinghorn of Norwich'* in 1855 during the whole of those 'latter years'.

It took some time for Simon to admit to himself that he had finally left Norwich. Soon after his removal the Chairman of the Norfolk and Norwich Literary Institution wrote to enquire whether he intended to reside permanently in London. Whatever reply he may have given it was not till two years later that the Institution appointed a new Librarian, John Quinton, in his place. On that occasion (20th October 1836) Thomas Brightwell proposed their thanks to Simon for his valuable services and that his name should stand as Honorary Librarian and Secretary with free enjoyment of the privileges of membership. The proposition was seconded by his one-time partner William Youngman and agreed to. His separation from the church of St Mary's was more painful and took longer to accomplish. On June 1st 1835 the St Mary's Church Meeting directed the Rev. William Brock to write and enquire when he intended to return to Norwich. An indefinite reply resulted in what Brock minuted as a 'long troublesome discussion'. Some members thought that if he did not return to perform his duties as a Deacon he should cease to hold that office. Brock wrote to him again with the result that he came down and attended the next Church Meeting on July 27th and 'answered for himself' which quelled his opponents for the time being.(1)

He appears to have maintained a pied-à-terre at Costessey at this time for in July 1836 Thomas Brightwell wrote to him there enquiring:

"Has the Black Jack got among your Turnips at Cossey? I am rearing some of the caterpillers to see what they are the larvae of. Is it a moth?"(2)

Simon was in Norwich again in November (1836) when
he attended a Church Meeting at St Mary's and argued
against a course of action which he feared might ultimately
lead to the adoption of the practice of Open Communion.
His associates in the church later alleged that during
Joseph Kinghorn's ministry and for some time afterwards he
had been a zealous advocate of Open Communion. By now however he felt it necessary to conform to his old master's
view and so took the opposite line.(3)

Three years passed before Simon's position at St
Mary's again came up for review. In December 1839 Joseph
Allen, another of the Deacons, who had moved to Camberwell,
wrote resigning his office. This immediately called in
question Simon's membership of the Diaconate since he had
been much longer absent. Brock was instructed to write
respectfully but firmly requesting his resignation. Simon
was entirely unwilling to resign,
"I have never," he wrote, "considered my removal from
Norwich as other than an experiment and now more than
ever since I left do I regard it but too probable that
I may feel it my duty, however reluctantly, to return".

Further, he put down the desire for his resignation
to the animosity towards him of James Cozens, though he
gave no reason for this opinion. Not unnaturally Brock
found his intransigence annoying. He wrote,
"This is the second time we have had our comfort interrupted by this very question".

Every one of his (Simon's) friends, wrote Brock,
disagreed with his refusal to resign and it would do him
credit to give up his determination. He did not. Another
year was allowed to pass but in March 1841 on the proposal
of none other than Josiah Fletcher the Church at St Mary's
terminated the membership of Simon and Emma Wilkin and a
number of other absentees, sending them 'letters of commen-
dation' to take to any church in which they might wish to
settle. By this act of the church Simon ceased to be a
member and Deacon of St Mary's, but not without protest.
He wrote to Brock and to the Deacons and at the June (1841)
Church Meeting his father-in-law, John Culley, pleaded that
the matter be reconsidered. The members expressed their
sympathy with John Culley's paternal feelings and avowed
their love for him and the Wilkins but were determined to
stand by what they had done. John Culley, it may be said,
did not share his son-in-law's views. He was a strong
supporter of William Brock and helped to persuade him to
stay in Norwich when, later in the year, he was invited to
go to London to be Secretary of the Baptist Missionary
Society.(1)

Simon's links with St Mary's were not wholly severed
since he remained a Trustee of the church's property, but
perhaps he would have given up his active opposition to
the course being taken there had not another protagonist
entered the lists. William Norton, a nephew of Emma's,
another of the Trustees of St Mary's property, had been
studying with Kinghorn at the time of his last illness.
In 1833 he had gone up to Stepney College but had not im-
bibed the preference for Open Communion existing among many
of the students there. He was determined to do all in his

power to prevent this practice being adopted at St Mary's
and he carried Simon with him. About March 1845 Brock
instituted a second monthly Communion Service to which he
admitted Christians who had not been baptised on profession
of their faith. This started a long course of disagreement
between William Norton and Simon Wilkin on the one hand and
the Trustees resident in Norwich on the other. More than
once Counsel's Opinion was sought. When a case was drawn
up by Norton, Counsel advised that there had been a breach
of trust; when a case was submitted by the Norwich Trustees
equally eminent Counsel opined that there was none. So
matters stood when William Brock left Norwich in 1848.
Despite these differences his pastorate at St Mary's had
been a happy and successful one and the membership of the
church had more than doubled since he came to Norwich.
      We have scant information about Simon's activities
after the move to Hampstead. His obituary in the proceedings of the Linnean Society says that commercial pursuits
prevented him keeping up an active connection with the
literary and scientific world, but there is not much
evidence of such pursuits. He seems to have acted as a
literary agent for Amelia Opie. In January 1843 she wrote
asking him to negotiate with Groves and Sons, booksellers
in the Borough, for a reprint of her works. They had
offered to undertake this giving her a number of copies.
She had consulted Josiah Fletcher who thought she should
have better renumeration. In February she wrote again to
say she would not part with her copyright but would agree
to Groves printing a duodecimo edition of her works, giving
her two sets and a small amount of money. In May she had
raised her sights -- five guineas and a dozen copies would
not be too much. She could not, she wrote, go about with
a donkey selling her copies. She feared she would get
nothing by the departed children of her brains. Some
arrangement was ultimately come to and in August (1843)
she wrote asking Simon to draw up an advertisement of the
proposed edition for the public papers.(4) Amelia afterwards said of this reprint --
   "I got no money whatever by it - only the pleasure of
   knowing that all mention of the *great name* , & other blem-
   ishes are to be expunged in the new edition."
      When her friend J.J. Gurney saw the advertisement
he wrote to her suggesting that what she had done infringed
an undertaking given when she joined the Society of Friends.
She wrote a long reply justifying her action. She had
promised, she said, never to write things of the same sort
again, nor had she done so. She believed simple moral
tales the best mode of instructing the young and the poor.
"And why did the blessed Saviour teach in parables?" Her
own books, "Which Friends never read, & know nothing about",
are moral tales and she has had many proofs that they have
occasionally done good.(5)
      In 1843 too the Wilkins became acquainted with Jo-
hann Gerhard Oncken of Hamburg who in that year enjoyed
the hospitality of Cossey Cottage, Hampstead. Oncken had
undergone an evangelical conversion during a previous
residence in London. He had come to a Baptist position
by his own study of the Scriptures and in 1834 he and six

106

others had been baptised in the Elbe by a visiting American minister and had formed the first German Baptist Church. Despite a measure of persecution numbers had grown steadily and in 1843 there were 273 baptisms. Following Oncken's visit to Hampstead Martin Wilkin was sent to his home in Hamburg to learn German, while Simon became Treasurer of the German Baptist Mission, raising money to assist Baptist churches on the continent.(6)

We get a glimpse of Simon Wilkin in these latter years in the diary of his niece Cecilia Lucy Brightwell, who recorded that he was in Norwich in August 1851 when he met the Borrows at her father's house in Surrey Street, not having seen George Borrow for twenty years past. On this occasion Borrow discoursed on his adventures in Hungary and remembered eating black cherries of fabulous size in an orchard on the slopes of the Tokay mountain. She also tells us that Simon called on Mr Husenbeth, the Roman Catholic Chaplain to the Jerninghams at Costessey, an enthusiastic antiquary and a man of letters with a wide variety of interests. Besides a *'Defence of the Creed and Discipline of the Catholic Church'*, he had written *'Original Songs adapted to German Melodies'*, a *'Guide for the Wine Cellar'*, and most recently *'Emblems of the Saints'* and was then engaged in translating the Vulgate into English. Pope Pius IX had recently conferred on him the degree of Doctor of Divinity and he proudly shewed Simon the ring given him on that occasion with an amethyst as large as a bean standing out, round and polished. He would, he said, have preferred an emerald but had to be satisfied with what had been given him.(7)

When Simon left Norwich he had taken with him some 5,000 letters and notes, the literary testament of the late Joseph Kinghorn. He was at first daunted with the prospect of reading and reducing this mass of material into a biography and he received little encouragement from London publishers whom he consulted. After he had finished work on his edition of Sir Thomas Browne he started on Kinghorn's legacy, destroying hundreds of letters as worthless. He found the work heavy and made little progress until Martin, who took a great interest in the letters, was old enough to take a major part of the work and the labour became 'a family compact'. In February 1855 'Joseph Kinghorn of Norwich' was completed and on 'a dark stormy afternoon, the ground covered with snow' Simon sat down to write the Preface which seems to have been his last literary labour. The work was then sent to Josiah Fletcher to print.(8)

Meanwhile (in 1849) George Gould had succeeded William Brock as pastor of St Mary's Baptist Church. He came as a recognised advocate of Open Communion and the church was moving towards that position. William Norton conducted a long correspondence with Gould in protest against this course of action. Both sides wished to have the legal aspects of the matter settled by arbitration but could not agree on the arrangements for doing so.

There had been, from the seventeenth century onwards, a diversity of practice on the Communion Question among the Baptist Churches though in Norfolk the Closed Table had prevailed. Now the tide was running against this view and a number of churches were changing their practice. In Norfolk the Great Ellingham church adopted Open Communion in 1854; that at Worstead in 1858. In March 1857 the church at St Mary's decided to adopt the practice of Open Communion. A year later, on May 13th 1858, Simon Wilkin, William Norton and two members of St Mary's who espoused Strict Communion filed an Information and Bill against George Gould and the remaining Trustees, alleging a breach of trust, seeking an injunction against the practice of Open Communion at St Mary's and asking for the removal of George Gould from being Minister and of the other defendants from being Trustees of the Church's property. Two more years elapsed before the matter could be brought to trial. On April 30th 1860 and for two subsequent days no less than six learned Counsel argued the case before the Master of Rolls. George Gould had spent much time during the interval in research into the history of the Baptist Churches and of Nonconformity generally, satisfying himself that the Strict Communion position was an innovation rather than otherwise. On the basis of his studies his Counsel was able to convince the Court and on May 28th (1860) the Master of the Rolls gave judgement, the essential part of his long disquisition being:

"that each Congregation was from the earliest time at liberty to regulate its practice, either to the Strict Communion or to the Free or Mixed Communion as it might seem best to such Congregation".

Thus Simon Wilkin's bid to tie the congregation at St Mary's to the line of conduct Joseph Kinghorn had favoured failed and the last thread of his influence in Norwich was broken. The Norfolk News, established in 1845 by a caucus of Norwich Dissenters to give publicity to their views, published the judgement at length, besides an extract from the Times on the case -- two and a half columns in all.

'The Master of the Rolls after all his research and with all his acuteness,' wrote the Times reporter, 'could not discover that actual baptism by immersion had been ever determined by Baptist authorities to be an indispensible condition of Baptist Communion'.

He went on to comment that the conduct of a case so apparently strange was forcibly illustrative of English feeling and habits. The judgement made it possible for Baptist churches to change their practice as to the Communion without fear of legal proceedings but it sharpened the division between those who wished to maintain a Closed Table and the rest -- a division which persists to the present day.

Two years after the judgement, on August 2nd 1862 Simon Wilkin died at Hampstead. His body was brought back to his birthplace and buried in Costessey churchyard.

Nearly a generation had passed since he left Norwich and almost all his close associates had died -- R.M. Bacon, his partner in the disastrous paper-mill business; all his brethren of the United Friar's Society; John Harvey, his collaborator in the Literary Institution; the local celebrities, J.J. Gurney and William Taylor; and Amelia Opie, who had been wont to consult him about her publications --

all gone and he himself almost forgotten. The old-
established Norwich newspapers scarcely noticed his death.
Only the editor of the Norfolk News remembered that he had
made a contribution to Norwich life which ought to be
recorded. He ordered a brief obituary notice, the writer
of which set down that during his (Simon's) residence in
Norwich he had been well known in connection with whatever
related to literature and science and had established the
Norfolk and Norwich Literary Institution and afterwards
the Museum, both of which were for a long time conducted
under his roof.

REFERENCES

1. St Mary's Church Book
2. Letters to S. Wilkin re Sir Thomas Browne, N.R.O.21278
3. St Mary's Chapel Case. Answer to amended Information
   and Bill, para.78
4. Wilkin Papers 139-44
5. Amelia Opie to J.J. Gurney, 23 February 1844 in
   Friends House Library
6. Dr Hans Luckey, *Johan Gerhard Oncken und die anfange des
   Deutschen Baptismus*. 1934, p.265
7. Diary of C.L. Brightwell, N.R.O.
8. M.H. Wilkin, *Joseph Kinghorn of Norwich*

Appendix   (Works printed by S. Wilkin)

Books and pamphlets printed by Simon Wilkin at
Norwich; a list compiled from the 'Colman Catalogue'
(Bibliotheca Norfolciencis, 1896) with additions.

1818

Norwich Guardians. A list of Persons resident in the
Great Ward of Conisford and receiving Out-door Relief from
the Corporation of Guardians on the 25th March 1818.
8vo. Norwich; Wilkin and Youngman

Norwich Guardians. A list of Persons resident in the
Great Northern Ward and receiving Out-door Relief from
the Corporation of Guardians on the 25th of March 1818.
8vo. Norwich; Wilkin and Youngman

Norwich Union Fire and Life Insurance Societies. Substance
of the Report of the London Committee of Investigation,
made at the City of London Tavern on the 25th September
1818.
15 pp. 8vo. Norwich; Wilkin and Youngman

1819

Alexander (Rev. John). An Address delivered on the
occasion of Laying the Foundation Stone of Prince's Street
Chapel. March 16th 1819.
15 pp. 12mo. Norwich; Wilkin and Youngman

Association of Manufacturers, Dyers and others concerned
in the various branches of the Manufactures of the City
of Norwich, for preventing frauds, embezzlements, abuses
and unlawful combinations.
24 pp. 8vo. Norwich; Wilkin and Youngman

Norwich Union Office for Insurance on Lives and Granting
or Purchasing Annuities, Endowments &c.
48 pp. 8vo. Norwich; Wilkin and Youngman

1820

Hull (Rev. William). The Duty of Christians towards Civil
Rulers. The Substance of a Discourse preached at the Old
Meeting, Norwich, February 6th 1820, on the Accession to
the Throne of these Realms, of his Majesty George IV.
33 pp. 8vo. Norwich; Wilkin and Youngman

Kinghorn (Rev. Joseph). A Defence of "Baptism a Term of
Communion" in answer to the Rev. Robert Hall's "Reply".
230 pp. 8vo. Norwich; Wilkin and Youngman

Yelloly (John, M.D.). Explanations relative to a proposed plan for forming a Collection of Books in aid of the
Norwich Public Library.
24 pp. 8vo. Norwich; Wilkin and Youngman

1821

Gibbs (Rev. George, Minister of St Clement's Baptist
Church, Norwich). A Defence of the Baptists, or the
Baptism of Believers by Immersion the only Baptism of the
Christian Dispensation.
8vo. Norwich; S. Wilkin

Hull (Rev. William). Children Admonished to Remember God.
A Discourse delivered at the Old Meeting, Norwich, October
4th 1821, on the occasion of the Death of Elizabeth Plat-
ford, a Child educated in the Sunday School belonging to
that Place of Worship.
24 pp. 12mo. Norwich; S. Wilkin

Norwich Union. Extracts from the Deed of Settlement of
the Norwich Union Fire Insurance Society, bearing date the
sixth day of August 1821 and enrolled in His Majesty's
High Court of Chancery.
27 pp. 12mo. Norwich; S. Wilkin

Rouillon (Monsieur De). Elements of French Conversation.
Norwich; S. Wilkin

1822

Norfolk and Norwich Literary Institution. A Sketch of the
Plan and Progress.
Norwich; S. Wilkin

Norfolk and Norwich Literary Institution, Laws of the; with
a list of Shareholders and Subscribers and the Officers
and Committee elected 22nd October 1822.
20 pp. Market Place, Norwich; S. Wilkin

1823

Disney (Henry Beverley, Trinity Pilot, Lowestoft). The

Voice of Truth, in Reply to a Pamphlet, entitled "A
Warning Voice to the projectors, subscribers and supporters of the Plan for making Norwich a Port"; with a
Chart of the coast and actual soundings &c.
20 pp. 8vo. Norwich; S. Wilkin

Evans (Lewis, M.D.). A letter to John Harvey on the
utility of the Infirmary for the diseases of the eyes
established at Norwich; by Dr Evans, Physician to the
Institution.
Norwich; S. Wilkin

Kinghorn (Rev. Joseph). The Argument in Support of Infant
Baptism from the Covenant of Circumcision, examined and
shewn to be invalid.
24 pp. 12mo. Norwich; S. Wilkin

Martineau (Harriet). Devotional Exercises, consisting of
reflections and prayers for the use of Young Persons: to
which is added a Treatise on the Lord's Supper, by a Lady.
125 pp. 12mo. Upper Haymarket, Norwich; S. Wilkin

Norfolk and Norwich Literary Institution, Catalogue of the
Library of,
Upper Haymarket, Norwich; S. Wilkin

Norwich Guardians. Report on the Proceedings on hearing
an Appeal between the Hamlets of Norwich and the Court of
Guardians, at an adjourned Quarter Sessions for the City
of Norwich, held the 9th and 10th of December 1822.
128 pp. 8vo. Norwich; S. Wilkin

Norwich Union Life Insurance Society. Report of Mr Morgan,
the Actuary, on the state of the Society in June 1822, and
resolutions approving the said report and declaring a
second bonus of 24 percent, passed at a General Meeting of
the Members held at the Society's Office on Monday the
28th July 1823.
15 pp. 12mo. Norwich; S. Wilkin

Rouillon (Monsieur De). Grammatical Institutes of the
French Language.
Norwich; S. Wilkin

Rouillon (Monsieur De). Analytical Table of Genders of
French Nouns.
Norwich; S. Wilkin

Turner (Charles). An Introduction to Arithmetic, for the
use of Pottergate Street House Academy, Norwich.
sm8vo. Norwich; S. Wilkin

Watts (Thomas). Catholicism Indefensible: or an Answer to
the Rev. J.A. Carr's Letter.
36 pp. 8vo. Norwich; S. Wilkin

1824

Beaumont (Rev. George). The Anti-Swedenborg - or a
Declaration of the principal errors and anti-scriptural
doctrines contained in the theological writings of Emmanuel
Swedenborg. Being the sustance of a lecture delivered at
Ebenezer Chapel, Sunday August 24th 1823 with considerable
additions.
156 pp. 12mo. London; Richard Baynes. Printed Norwich;
S. Wilkin.

Catalogue of the Norwich (Penny) Library for Working People
at Mr Dann's, St Michael's Coslany.
12 pp. 12mo. Norwich; S. Wilkin

Copland (W. of Sharrington, Norfolk). A letter to the
Rev. C.D. Brereton in reply to his "Observations on the
Administration of the Poor Laws in Agricultural Districts",
containing also, Some remarks upon his Attack on the
Magistrates of the County, and tracing the Great Increase
of Pauperism to its Proper Source.
126 pp. 8vo. Norwich; S. Wilkin

Kinghorn (Rev. Joseph). An Address to a Friend on Church
Communion; with an Appendix containing a Brief Statement
of the Sentiments of the Baptists on the Ordinance of
Baptism.
38 pp. 12mo. Norwich; S. Wilkin

Kinghorn (Rev. Joseph). Clavis Pentateuchi; sive Analysis
omnium vocum Hebraicarum suo ordine in Pentateucho Moseos
occurentium, una cum versione Latina et Anglica. Auctore
Jacobo Robertson S.T.D. Ling. Oriental, in Academia Edin-
burgena Professore. Editio altera: ex recensione Josephi
Kinghorn.
714 pp. 8vo. Norvici: Typis excudebat, Simon Wilkin

Opie (Amelia). The Negro Boy's Tale, a Poem addressed to
Children.
16 pp. sm8vo. London; Harvey and Darton. Printed, Norwich;
S. Wilkin

Scripture Catechism; being a series of Questions with
References to the Scriptures instead of Answers. To which
is prefixed a Chronological Table of the whole Scripture
History, comprising a Calendar of Christ's Ministry.
12mo. Norwich; S. Wilkin

1825

Denny (Henry). Monographia Pselaphidarum et Scydmaenidarum
Britanniae: or an Essay on the British Species of the
Genera Pselaphus of Herbst and Scydmaenus of Latreille.
8vo. Norwich; S. Wilkin

Gurney (Anna, of Northrepps). On the Means of Assistance

in Cases of Shipwreck.
40 pp. 8vo. Norwich; S. Wilkin

Horae Feriatae, or a Nest of Eaglets lately hatched at
Mile End, Eaton, Norwich.
26 pp. 12mo. Norwich; S. Wilkin

Kinghorn (Rev. Joseph). Considerations addressed to the
Eclectic Reviewer, in defence of those who maintain that
baptism should precede communion; occasioned by his
"Address to Correspondents" in the Eclectic Review for
Dec. 1824
38 pp. 8vo. Norwich; S. Wilkin

Norfolk and Norwich Literary Institution, Second Catalogue
of the Library of. May 1825.
Norwich; S. Wilkin

Opie (Amelia). Illustrations of Lying in all its Branches.
Two Volumes.
London; Longman, Hurst, Orme, Brown and Green. Printed,
Norwich; S. Wilkin

Opie (Amelia). Tales of the Pemberton Family; for the use
of Children.
12mo. London; Harvey and Darton. Printed Norwich; S. Wilkin

Rouillon (Monsieur De). Voyage de Polyclète, ou Lettres
Romains. Abrégé de l'ouvrage original de M. Le Baron de
Théis. À l'usage de la Jeunesse.
472 pp. 8vo. London; chez J. Souter, et Treutel, Wurtz & Co.
Printed, Norwich; S. Wilkin

1826

Borrow (George Henry). Romantic Ballads, translated from
the Danish; and Miscellaneous Pieces.
8vo. Norwich; S. Wilkin

Disney (Henry Beverley). Important Considerations on the
Subject of "Norwich a Port".
24 pp. 8vo. Norwich; S. Wilkin

Martineau (Harriet). Addresses with Prayers and Original
Hymns for the use of Families and Schools, by a Lady.
152 pp. 12mo. London; Rowland Hunter. Printed Nov. 1 1826,
Norwich; S. Wilkin

Norwich and Lowestoft Navigation. Abstract of the Minutes
of Evidence taken before a Committee of the House of Commons, during the Session of 1826, on the Bill for making a
Navigable Communication for Ships and other Vessels, between
the City of Norwich and the Sea at or near Lowestoft.
56 pp. 8vo. Norwich; S. Wilkin

The Sabbath. The Institution and Observance of the Sabbath

considered.
12mo. Norwich; S. Wilkin

Simpson (William). Statement of the Facts which occurred
in the late affair between Mr Bulkeley, of the 40th Regiment, and Mr William Simpson.
16 pp. 8vo. Norwich; S. Wilkin

Stereotyping, Extract of a Letter on.
12 pp. 8vo. Norwich; S. Wilkin

1827

Kinghorn (Rev. Joseph). Arguments against the practice of
Mixed Communion on the Plan of the Apostolic Church; with
Preliminary Observations on Rev. R. Hall's Reasons for
Christian, in opposition to Party Communion.
80 pp. 12mo. Norwich; S. Wilkin

Kinghorn (Rev. Joseph). Sketch of the Life of the Rev.
Isaac Slee; with an Extract from his Farewell Sermon, on
his Resigning the Perpetual Curacy of Plumpton in Cumber-
land, in consequence of becoming a Baptist.
24 pp. 12mo. Norwich; S. Wilkin

1828

Alexander (Rev. John). A letter, dated March 10 1828,
addressed to the Church and Congregation connected with
Prince's Street Chapel, Norwich.
12 pp. 12mo. Norwich; S. Wilkin

Brightwell (Thomas, F.L.S.). Journal of a Tour made by a
Party of Friends in the Autumn of 1825, through Belgium,
up the Rhine &c.
8vo. Norwich; S. Wilkin

Horae Feriatae or the Eaglet. By the Pupils at Mile-end
School, Eaton, Norwich. Number II. March 27th 1828.
142 pp. 12mo. Norwich; S. Wilkin

Opie (Amelia). Detraction Displayed.
Norwich; S. Wilkin

Taylor (William). Historic Survey of German Poetry. Vol. I.
8vo. London; Treuttel & Wurtz, Treuttel jun. & Richter.
Printed, Norwich; S. Wilkin

1829

Guide to Young Persons in the Holy Scriptures.
Norwich; S. Wilkin

Gurney (Joseph John). Some Account of John Stratford, who
was Executed after the last Assizes for the City of Norwich

for the Crime of Murder. By one of his Fellow-Citizens.
15 pp. 12mo. Norwich; S. Wilkin

Kinghorn (Rev. Joseph). Remarks on a Country Clergyman's
attempt to explain the nature of the visible church, the
Divine Commission of the Clergy, &c., being a defence of
Dissenters in general, and of Baptists in particular, on
New Testament principlals.
36 pp. 12mo. Norwich; S. Wilkin

Taylor (William). Historic Survey of German Poetry. Vol. II.
8vo. London; Treuttel & Wurtx, Treuttel jun. & Richter.
Printed, Norwich; S. Wilkin

1830

Geary (William). An earnest Appeal to the Weavers of
Norwich, on passing events of the present awful Crisis.
12 pp. 12mo. Norwich; S. Wilkin

Joseph (Henry Samuel). Reasons for renouncing Judaism and
embracing Christianity, being an Address to the Children
of the House of Israel.
8vo. Norwich; S. Wilkin

Meteyard (W.H., B.C.L.). Some Remarks on a Pamphlet
entitled "Thoughts submitted to the Employers of Labour
&c.", by John Weyland Esq. M.P., F.R.S.
22 pp. 8vo. Norwich; S. Wilkin

Norfolk and Norwich Museum. Sixth Annual Meeting on Wednesday 28th November 1830. Report of the Committee &c.
Norwich; Wilkin and Fletcher

Taylor (William). Historic Survey of German Poetry.
Vol. III.
8vo. London; Treuttel & Wurtz, Treuttel jun. & Richter.
Printed, Norwich; Wilkin and Fletcher

1831

Adams (Samuel, of Swanington). A letter to the Right
Honourable Lord Suffield on the Degraded Condition of the
Labouring Poor occasioned by the modern administration of
the Poor Laws.
44 pp. 8vo. Norwich; Wilkin and Fletcher

Burrows (G.C.). Plain Sense and Reason. Letters to the
Present Generation on the Unrestrained Use of Modern
Machinery, particularly addressed to my Countrymen and
Fellow Citizens.
30 pp. 8vo. Norwich; Wilkin and Fletcher

Watts (Thomas). The Present Evils and Alarming Prospects
of the Agricultural Population, with a safe, easy and

effectual Remedy.
32 pp. 8vo. Norwich; Wilkin and Fletcher

1832

Alexander (Rev. John). The Mourning Congregation reminded
of the Work of their deceased Minister. A Funeral Sermon
preached in St Mary's Meeting House, Norwich on September
9th 1832.
25 pp. 8vo. Norwich; Wilkin and Fletcher

Burrows (G.C.). Letters to the Present Generation on the
Unrestrained Use of Modern Machinery. (Second Issue).
30 pp. 8vo. Norwich; Wilkin and Fletcher

Gurney (Joseph John). Hints on the Portable Evidence of
Christianity.
12mo. Norwich; Wilkin and Fletcher

Gurney (Joseph John). Terms of Union. Remarks addressed
to the Members of the British and Foreign Bible Society.
46 pp. 8vo. Norwich; Wilkin and Fletcher

Norfolk and Norwich Literary Institution, Appendix to the
Second Catalogue of the Library of.
Norwich; Wilkin and Fletcher

1833

Hart (Rev. Richard, Vicar of Catton). Medulla Conciliorum
Magnae Britanniae et Hiberniae, ab an. dom. 446 ad an. dom.
1548.
Norvici; Wilkin and Fletcher

Joseph Kinghorn, The Catalogue of the Entire Library of;
with an engraving of Kinghorn and a select catalogue of
new and second-hand books offered by Wilkin and Fletcher.
80 pp. 8vo. Norwich; Wilkin and Fletcher

1834

Opie (Amelia). Lays for the Dead.
12mo. London; Longman, Rees, Orme, Brown, Green and Longman.
Printed, Norwich; Wilkin and Fletcher

Youngman (William). The Capacities and Responsibilities of
Man, in relation to the Moral Government of God, examined.
A Letter to the Committee of the Congregational Library,
occasioned by their publication of Dr Wardlaw's Lectures
on Christian Ethics.
46 pp. 8vo. Norwich; Wilkin and Fletcher

UNDATED

Mackay (Sampson Arnold). Mythological Astronomy. Part
the second. Containing the Astronomical Explanation of
the Hindoo Mythology and their Celebrated Mystical
Numbers &c.
23 pp. sm8vo. Norwich; Wilkin and Fletcher

Mackie (S.). A Catalogue of Fruit and Forest Trees, ever-
green and flowering Shrubs, Plants, flower seeds &c. sold
by S. Mackie, Nursery, Norwich.
144 pp. 12mo. Norwich; S. Wilkin

Unpublished sources

(N.R.O. means Norfolk Record Office)
C.L. Brightwell MS 69, N.R.O.
Fletcher Family Papers belonging to Mrs Jill Paine
H.E. Gunton. Chronological Costessey. Typescript in
Norwich Local History Library
Gurney's Bank Ledgers at Barclay's Bank, Norwich
Kinghorn Letters in possession of the author
Linnean Society - Smith Papers
London Missionary Society. Committee Minutes, at School of
Oriental and African Studies, London
M.J. Muncaster. The 19th Century Epidemics of Cholera in
Norfolk and Norwich. Typescript in Norwich Local History
Library
Norfolk and Norwich Literary Institution. Minute Book
Norfolk and Norwich Museum. Acquisitions Book at Norwich
Castle Museum
Norfolk and Norwich Museum. Committee Minutes at Norwich
Castle Museum
Norwich Public Library. Minute Book
Norwich United Friars Society Transactions. N.R.O.
H. Crabb Robinson Collection, in Dr William's Library,
London
St Mary's Baptist Church, Norwich. Second & Third Church
Books. N.R.O.
R. Stedman. Vox Populi, Typescript in Norwich Local History
Library
Wilkin Papers. N.R.O.
Notes on Wilkin Papers destroyed by bombing; cited as
'C.B.J. notes'.

Bibliography

Allen, Mea. The Hookers of Kew. London. 1967
Bidwell, W.H. Annals of an East Anglian Bank. Norwich. 1900
Binfield, Clyde. So Down to Prayers. London. 1977
Birks, T.R. Memoir of the Rev. Edward Bickersteth. London.
1852
Birrell, C.M. Life of William Brock D.D. London. 1878
Brightwell, C.L. Life of Mr Brightwell of Norwich.
Norwich. 1896
Brightwell, C.L. Memorials of the Life of Amelia Opie.
Norwich. 1854
Braithwaite, J.B. Memoirs of Joseph John Gurney. Norwich.
1855
Browne, Sir Thomas's Works. Bohn's Edition. London. 1852

Chambers, John. General History of the County of Norfolk.
Norwich. 1829
Clark, E. Kitson. History of 100 years life of Leeds
Philosophical and Literary Society. Leeds. 1924
Colman, Helen Caroline. A Memoir of Jeremiah James Colman.
London 1905
Coupland, Sir Reginald. Wilberforce. London. 1945
Cozens-Hardy and Kent. Mayors of Norwich 1403-1835.
Norwich. 1938

Dictionary of National Biography
Dictionary of Scientific Biography. New York. 1971-1976
Digest of Evidence taken before His Majesty's Municipal
Corporation Commissioners at the Guildhall in the City of
Norwich. 1834

Freeman, John. Life of the Rev. William Kirby. London. 1852

Gillen, Mollie. Royal Duke: Augustus Fredrick, Duke of
Sussex. London. 1976
Gould, George. Open Communion and the Baptists of Norwich.
Norwich. 1860
Gould, George. Sermons and Addresses with a Memoir by
G.P. Gould. London. 1883
Greeves, J.W. Reply to Mr Geary's Appeal to the Weavers of
Norwich. Norwich. 1830
Grigor, James. The Eastern Arboretum. London. 1841.
Grunebaum-Ballin. Henri Grégoire, L'Ami des Hommes de
toutes les couleurs

Keynes, Sir Geoffrey. Bibliography of Sir Thomas Browne.
Cambridge. 1924

Kirby, William (& William Spence). An Introduction to
Entomology. London. 1818
Kitson, S.D. Life of John Sell Cotman. London. 1937
Korngold, Ralph. Citizen Toussaint. London. 1945

Linnean Society. Journal of Proceedings. Vol. VII
Luckey, Dr Hans. Johan Gerhardt Oncken und die Anfange
des Deutschen Baptismus. Kassel. 1934

Martineau, Harriet. Autobiography. London. 1877
Mottram, R.H. John Crome of Norwich. London. 1932
Mottram, R.H. Success to the Mayor. London. 1937

Newspapers: Bury and Norwich Post
           East Anglian, or Norfolk, Suffolk & Cambridge-
           shire, Norwich, Lynn & Yarmouth Herald
           Iris
           Norfolk Chronicle
           Norwich Mercury
           Times
Norfolk and Norwich Naturalists Society. Transactions.
Vol. X & XI
Norgate, T.B. History of Costessey. Aylsham. 1972
Norgate, T.B. History of Taverham. Aylsham. 1969
Norton, William. Baptist Chapel, St. Mary's. Norwich. The
Suit - Attorney General v. Gould and others. London. 1860
Norwich election poll books

Ordish, G. John Curtis and the Pioneering of Pest Control.
London. 1974

Pollock, John. Wilberforce. London. 1977

Royle, Edward. Victorian Infidels. Manchester. 1974

St. Mary's Chapel Case. Answer to amended Information & Bill
Schofield, R.E. The Lunar Society of Birmingham. Oxford. 1963
Shaffer, E.S. Kubla Khan and the Fall of Jerusalem.
Cambridge. 1973
Stoker, D. Early History of Paper-making in Norfolk. Norfolk
Archaeology, Vol. XXXVI
Stoughton, John. History of Religion in England.
Vol. VI & VII. London. 1901

Vandercook, J.W. Black Majesty. Life of Christophe, King of
Haiti. New York. 1928
Venn, J.A. Alumni Cantabrigiensis. Cambridge. 1954

Wernerian Natural History Society, Memoirs of. Edinburgh.
1811
Wilkin, Martin Hood. Joseph Kinghorn of Norwich. Norwich.
1855
Woodforde, James. Diary of a Country Parson. Ed. John
Beresford. Oxford. 1831
Wright, G. A list of Subscribers to the Manchester
Sufferers. Norwich. 1819

Index

Dalton, John, 84
Daniel, E.T., 57n; S., 13
Darken, John, 94
Darwin, Erasmus, 84, 85
Davey, Jonathon, 14, 90;
  Emma, 90
David, Mr (upholsterer),
  48; Mrs, 1, 5, 40
Davy, Sir Humphrey, 84
Dawbarn, Richard, 40
Day, Starling, 93
Denny, George, 61; Henry,
  60, 61, 113
Derby, 98
Dereham, 96, 98
Dictionary of National
  Biography, 1, 50, 61, 82,
  104
Dieppe, 34
Disney, Henry Beverley, 62,
  111, 114
Donkin, Bryan, 25
Dore, Rev. James, 15
Dover, 57; John, 73
Dowson, John Withers, 49
Drummond, Rev. Thomas, 60
Duncon, Samuel, 83
Dugdale, Sir William, 86
Durrant, Mrs, 7; William,
  2, 5

Eagle, William, 77, 78
East Anglian Herald, 65,
  70-78, 96, 97
East India Company, 94
Eastern Counties News-
  papers, 79
Eaton School, 91, 114, 115
Eaton, Thomas, 42, 44, 46
Ebenezer Chapel, Norwich,
  51, 113
Edinburgh, 24, 50, 65;
  University, 6, 53
Education, 3, 7, 8, 13, 14,
  31, 69, 75, 91
Eichhorn (German theolo-
  gian), 12
Elba, 29, 34
Elections, 59, 68, 69, 74,
  75, 77, 78, 100
Elswick Leadworks (New-
  castle), 24
Entomology, 11, 16-18, 22,
  23, 32, 39, 53, 54, 60,
  62, 84
Erskine, Lord, 22
Evans, Dr L., 53, 112

Evelyn, John, 86
Evolution, 85
Executions, 56, 67, 68

Favell, Mr (London Book-
  seller), 21
Fireworks, 9, 77
Firth, William, 30
Fishwick, Richard, 24
Fletcher, Josiah, 50, 56,
  59, 63, 69, 79, 86, 87,
  94, 99, 101, 102, 105-
  107; Sarah (nee Williams),
  102
Forby, Rev. Robert, his
  Vocabulary of East Anglia,
  86
Forster, Dr Samuel, 24, 31;
  Miss, 31
Foster, Alderman, 52; F and
  Unthank, 40
Foster's Bank (Cambridge),
  34, 64
Fourdrinier (Papermaking
  machine), 25
France, 8, 9, 24, 29, 32-34,
  57
French National Assembly, 28,
  33; Revolution, 8, 54, 90
Friends, Society of, 13, 65,
  106
Fuller, Rev. Andrew, 3

Game Laws, 69
Geary, William, 68, 116
Geological Society, Trans-
  actions of, 84
George III, King, 52; IV,
  43, 63, 68, 72
German Baptist Mission, 107
Germany, 24, 57, 90, 107
Gibbs, Rev. George, 44, 111
Glasgow, 64
Glastonbury, 15, 16
Gloucester, 16; H.R.H. Duke
  of, 52
Glover, Rev. G., 27
Gooderson, John, 97, 98
Goose, Edward, 92, 93;
  Jacob, 92
Gould, Rev. George, 107.
  108
Goulty, Rev. John Nelson,
  33, 34, 38, 50
Gowing, Mr (of Hellesdon),
  73
Grant, Robert M.P., 68, 69,
  74-77

Printed in Great Britain by Headley Brothers Ltd The Invicta Press Ashford Kent and London